AIRCRAFT OF THE ACES
114
Ki-61 AND Ki-100 ACES

SERIES EDITOR TONY HOLMES

114

AIRCRAFT OF THE ACES

Nicholas Millman

Ki-61 AND Ki-100 ACES

OSPREY
PUBLISHING

Dedication

For Mike Goodwin 1960-2015

First published in Great Britain in 2015 by Osprey Publishing

PO Box 883, Oxford, OX1 9PL, UK

PO Box 3985, New York, NY 10185-3985, USA

E-mail: info@ospreypublishing.com

Osprey Publishing, part of Bloomsbury Publishing Plc

A CIP catalogue record for this book is available from the British Library

ISBN: 978 1 78096 295 5
PDF e-book ISBN: 978 1 78096 296 2
e-Pub ISBN: 978 1 78096 297 9

Edited by Tony Holmes
Cover Artwork by AviationArt.Aero
Aircraft Profiles and Scale Drawings by Ronnie Olsthoorn
Index by Alison Worthington
Originated by PDQ Digital Media Solutions, UK
Printed in China through World Print Limited

15 16 17 18 19   10 9 8 7 6 5 4 3 2 1

Osprey Publishing supports the Woodland Trust, the UK's leading woodland conservation charity. Between 2014 and 2018 our donations will be spent on their Centenary Woods project in the UK.

www.ospreypublishing.com

Acknowledgements

The author gratefully acknowledges the valued assistance of the following contributors – Luud Baier, Daniel Cox, Darryl Ford, Mike Goodwin, Isamu Ichige, Tetsuya Inoue, Dr Yasuho Izawa, Susumu Kajinami, Tokuko Kikuchi, James F Lansdale, James I Long, Don Marsh, Lex McAulay, Carl Molesworth, Keishiro Nagao, Giuseppe Picarella, Ronnie Olsthoorn, Mitsui Oyake, Cris Shapan, Fumisuke Shono, Takeo Tagata, Goro Takeda, Akio Takehashi and Hiroshi Umemoto. Any errors or misinterpretations are the author's sole responsibility.

Front Cover

On 22 December 1943 Ki-61 Hiens of the 68th Sentai intercepted B-25s of the 348th Bombardment Group as they made a low-level attack against the airstrips at Wewak and Boram, in New Guinea. Sgt Susumu Kajinami was one of seven 2nd Chutai pilots in action that day, flying as wingman to MSgt Matsui. After attacking two B-25s, Kajinami became separated from his leader and pursued one of the American bombers alone;

'From behind, I was chasing the fleeing B-25 along the coastline at very low altitude. The familiar shape of the bomber, painted in matt green or brown colour, got bigger and bigger in my sight. I fired both my 12.7 mm fuselage cannon, targeting between the left engine and inner wing, very close to her so I could clearly see the bullets sparking on the B-25. The upper panel of the engine nacelle broke off and flew away under my six-one. After a while the engine started to pour black smoke and she turned to the right and climbed towards the mountains. When she climbed to 300 m I fired again at the burning engine. At that time I saw three black figures bail out of the B-25. When the third figure passed away behind me the B-25 became a fireball and crashed into the jungle near the shore in a pillar of red fire.'

Sgt Kajinami's victim was probably B-25D-1 41-30080 *Little Stinky* of the 501st Bombardment Squadron. Its pilot, 1Lt E E Bailey, miraculously survived the crash, in the vicinity of Annanberg, and managed to reach the safety of Australian troops. However, the rest of the crew were never seen again (*Cover artwork by AviationArt.Aero*)

CONTENTS

INTRODUCTION

The Kawasaki Ki-61 'Hien' ('Swallow in Flight' – Allied codename 'Tony') or Type 3 single-seat fighter was the only Japanese inline-engined (liquid-cooled) operational fighter to serve in World War 2. However, it was not the first inline-engined fighter to serve in the Dai-Nippon Teikoku Rikugun Kokutai (the Imperial Japanese Army Air Force or IJAAF).

The aircraft section of KK Kawasaki Zosensho, which began production in Kobe in 1919, had specialised in aircraft designs using imported German technology and licence-built inline-engines since 1926, when it commenced production of the Army Type 89 Heavy Bomber (Kawasaki-Dornier Do N). Licence rights to manufacture BMW water-cooled engines had been awarded to Japan, then an Allied nation, as part of German reparations following World War 1.

In 1928 Kawasaki produced the experimental KDA-3 parasol wing fighter based on the Dornier Do H Falke and powered by a Hispano-Suiza 300 hp engine (for which Mitsubishi held the import and production rights), hoping to win an IJAAF contract in competition with Mitsubishi and Nakajima parasol designs. Despite rejection of the KDA-3 by the IJAAF in favour of the Nakajima design (which became the Type 91 fighter), Kawasaki persevered with the inline engine and, in 1930, its KDA-5 biplane fighter was accepted by the IJAAF as its Type 92 biplane fighter.

A fast 199 mph biplane, the Type 92 was designed by Dr Richard Vogt, Kawasaki's Chief Designer, and Takeo Doi, who would feature prominently in designing later Kawasaki fighters. The KDA-5 pioneered an all-metal construction, with very carefully finished alloy skin and fabric covering that was a hallmark of Kawasaki manufacture. The engine initially fitted was a Kawasaki licence-built version of the 500 hp BMW VI, but after 1933 a version of the BMW VII was used instead. The engine was capable of producing more cruising power at lower rpm, utilising a reduction gear to allow its maximum output to be increased to 750 hp.

A total of 385 Type 92 aircraft were built for the IJAAF, seeing service in Manchuria and China from 1932 to 1935. Despite being faster and possessing a greater rate of climb than the Nakajima-built Type 91, the Type 92 was not popular with pilots, who found it unstable during takeoff and landing, or groundcrews, who found the engine difficult to access and maintain.

In 1933, at the behest of the IJAAF, Kawasaki embarked on the design of the Ki-5 – a radical monoplane fighter intended to replace the Type 92. The Ki-5, which incorporated a fully spatted undercarriage and inverted gull wing, was powered by a Kawasaki-built 850 hp Ha-9-I engine enclosed in a streamlined cowling. This engine was an experimental design BMW IX that Kawasaki undertook to develop to production status. Its engineers focused on improving the supercharger to increase power and altitude performance, as well as making it more reliable. The Ha-9-I marked Kawasaki's emergence as an aero-engine developer in its own right.

However, numerous issues with the Ki-5, including a lack of in-flight stability, engine vibration and cooling problems, led to it being shelved in preference to further development of the Type 92. This resulted in production of the later Type 95, or Ki-10, biplane fighter. Powered by the 800 hp Ha-9-II Ko 12-cylinder vee engine – practically a BMW IX de-rated to improve reliability – the Ki-10 was accepted by the IJAAF in 1937 and served long enough to be allocated the Allied reporting name 'Perry'.

Although the Ki-5 had failed to enter operational service, manufacture and testing of the prototype provided Kawasaki with valuable experience in monoplane fighter design. A similar civil development that had been built in parallel – the C-5 – was to achieve fame by setting several speed and distance records whilst being flown by its owners, the newspaper *Asahi Shimbun*.

Kawasaki's next fighter design began to show the first vestiges of the eventual Ki-61 configuration and wing planform. Work on the experimental Ki-28 commenced in November 1935 in anticipation of an IJAAF competition announced in 1936. This aircraft was again powered by the Ha-9-II Ko engine. Up against the radial-engined Mitsubishi Ki-33 and Nakajima Ki-27 (the latter eventually codenamed 'Nate' by the Allies – see *Aircraft of the Aces 103 – Ki-27 'Nate' Aces* for further details), the Ki-28 demonstrated sparkling performance in speed, acceleration and climb. Although it had a wider turn radius, the Ki-28's higher speed ensured that the aircraft could travel 360 degrees in the same lapsed time as the other fighters. The Kawasaki machine could not cut inside the turns of the Ki-33 and Ki-27, however, and with an almost obsessive doctrinal priority on manoeuvrability and turn radius, the IJAAF rejected this promising design.

After the failure of the Ki-28, but still persevering with aircraft designs powered by liquid-cooled engines, Kawasaki turned its attention to gaining a production licence from Daimler-Benz to manufacture its respected DB 600 and DB 601 engines in Japan. This move was forced on Kawasaki for two reasons – BMW's abandonment of liquid-cooled engine development and the fact that the Ha-9-I had reached the end of its life.

In March 1938 the company secured a licence with high hopes that it could interest the IJAAF in initiating suitable design projects to exploit the new powerplant. Eventually, in February 1940, drawing on doctrinal lessons learned from aerial combat during the Nomonhan Incident with the Soviet Union, the IJAAF issued a requirement for Kawasaki to build a prototype experimental heavily armed fighter, which would become the Ki-60, and a 'lighter' general-purpose experimental fighter, which would become the Ki-61. The design of the Ki-60 was to emphasise speed, dive and climb performance, whilst the Ki-61 was planned to deliver the more general-purpose offensive capability required for the recently established doctrine of 'aerial exterminating action' (see *Aircraft of the Aces 103*). In fact the early versions of the Ki-61 had a higher loaded weight (2950 kg) than the prototype of the Ki-60 (2750 kg).

In April 1940 Kawasaki obtained the rights to manufacture the latest version of the Daimler-Benz engine, the DB 601A, with blueprints and pattern engines arriving from Germany that same year. The first Kawasaki-built DB 601A, designated the Ha-40, was available from July 1941, and by November it had passed all ground-running tests. Kawasaki, however, struggled with the responsibility of developing both the home-manufactured engine and the airframe design that it was intended to power. This resulted in a lengthy delay in the fighter's introduction to service. An irony lay in the fact that the ultimate – and arguably most successful – development of the Ki-61 would be the radial-engined Ki-100, which was the product of expediency rather than design.

The Ha-40 inverted-vee engine that would power the Ki-61 (an imported DB 601 was installed in the prototype Ki-60) was slightly lighter than the DB 601, but more powerful – it was rated at 1175 hp. Kawasaki had been unsuccessful in gaining licence manufacturing rights for the DB 601's all-important Bosch fuel injection system, so it had to incorporate a Mitsubishi-designed alternative instead. This proved effective enough, but in frontline service various engine-related problems with the Ki-61, which were magnified in the unforgiving environments to which it was deployed, were to ultimately blight the aircraft's operational record.

CHAPTER ONE

A DIFFICULT BIRTH

The three Ki-60 heavy fighter prototypes. The Ki-60 is sometimes described as the forerunner to the Ki-61, but the two designs were initiated in parallel to meet different specifications. Development of the Ki-60 was given priority, although it was subsequently terminated because of the aircraft's disappointing performance, dangerous spin characteristics and a lack of manoeuvrability. The more promising Ki-61 design was concentrated on instead (*San Diego Air & Space Museum*)

The development of the Ki-60 heavy fighter, of which three prototype examples were built, was given priority over the Ki-61 design. This was fortuitous because it enabled Takeo Doi and his design team to work through the shortcomings that soon became apparent with the Ki-60 design and to incorporate that experience in improving the Ki-61. The Ki-60's disappointing performance, dangerous spin characteristics and radical lack of manoeuvrability led to abandonment of the project. Indeed, the heavy fighter concept ultimately proved to be a blind alley in terms of Japanese fighter development and doctrine, not least because of the entrenched preference for traditional dogfighting manoeuvrability throughout the IJAAF.

Nakajima's more successful heavy fighter competitor, the Ki-44, achieved limited production status, although it too was regarded with suspicion and disliked by many IJAAF pilots (see *Aircraft of the Aces 100 – Ki-44 'Tojo' Aces of World War 2* for further details). Attention was now focused on the more conventional and promising Ki-61, Kawasaki planning on combining the speed, climb and dive performance of the heavy fighter concept with an acceptable level of manoeuvrability. The Ki-61 would be no aerobat like the Ki-27 or Nakajima Ki-43 Hayabusa (Peregrine Falcon), Allied reporting name 'Oscar' (see *Aircraft of the Aces 85 – Ki-43 'Oscar' Aces of World War 2* for further details), but its other flight characteristics, protection and armament were expected to more than compensate for that quality.

Much has been made of the similarity of the Ki-61 to Heinkel's He 100, three Block II A-0 examples of which were imported by Japan in the summer of 1940. The negotiations to obtain these aircraft had begun in November 1938, with drawings of an earlier version of the He 100 being passed on to a Japanese trade delegation a month later – one of them labelled as a Japanese version designated 'He 113'. In reality, the basic configuration of the Ki-61 had already been created in the fixed undercarriage Ki-28, which was flying in competition with other potential IJAAF fighter designs nearly two years earlier.

The Ki-61 is often characterised as a copy of Germany's Heinkel He 100 because of superficial similarities. However, the basic Ki-61 airframe was developed from the Kawasaki Ki-28 designed more than two years earlier. The He 100 was imported to Japan by the IJNAF with the intention of licence-building the type, and Kawasaki had access to an example during Ki-61 development. Some technical aspects of the He 100 were studied and influenced the design of the Ki-61 while other details were used and improved upon (*via Robert Forsyth*)

Also, initial interest in the He 100 was primarily from the Imperial Japanese Naval Air Force (IJNAF), and there is evidence of plans to build the type under licence – one of the imported He 100s undertook propeller vibration tests at the Naval Air Arsenal in Yokosuka. However, there is little doubt that technical aspects of the He 100 design were studied, utilised and/or improved upon by Kawasaki's Takeo Doi and Shin Owada in the design of the Ki-61, especially the mounting of the DB 601 engine to the airframe. These included the cowl structure, engine mounts and improved versions of the external cover plates over the engine mounting pins. The Kawasaki design team also incorporated scaled-down versions of the He 100's steam separator tanks to replace the swirl chambers usually attached to the coolant outlet ports of the DB 601. However, the Ki-61 employed a large fixed radiator beneath the rear fuselage, in a configuration similar to that of the P-51 Mustang.

The Ki-61 superficially resembled an enlarged version of the He 100, but it was by no means a copy. Instead, the Japanese fighter incorporated many advanced and superior features that were not a part of the German design.

The Ki-60 gets attention during test flights. The domestic Ha-40 engine fitted to the Ki-61 was lighter and more powerful than the imported Daimler-Benz DB 601 installed in the Ki-60. It was also fitted with a Mitsubishi fuel injection system rather than the Bosch system of the imported engine (*San Diego Air & Space Museum*)

The prototype Ki-61 (c/n 6101) was completed in December 1941, this aircraft being the first of 12 experimental prototypes to be manufactured and tested (c/n 6101-6112) through to July 1942, culminating in the manufacture of the first production model (c/n 6113) in August 1942.

FIRST ENCOUNTER

In April 1942 during the Doolittle Raid on Tokyo, US aircrew got their first glimpse of the sleek fighter that they would later tussle with so fiercely in the skies over New Guinea. At the time of the raid only five Ki-61 prototypes had been constructed (c/n 6101-6105), these aircraft being subjected to tests and trials by the Army Flight Test Centre at Fussa.

On 18 April 1942 Major Yoshitsugu Aramaki and WO Ryozaburo Umekawa of the Flight Test Centre had been flying the second and third Ki-61 prototypes in gunnery trials from Mito airfield, and were relaxing on the ground smoking cigarettes, when they were alerted to the raid. Through binoculars, they spotted a medium-sized aircraft with stars on its wings at an altitude of about 650 ft, and both pilots immediately decided to take off in an attempt to intercept it. However, the armourer officer, Capt Hashimoto, warned them that the two Hien prototypes were only loaded with practice ammunition of a non-explosive type, and he would need about 30 minutes to re-arm the aircraft with explosive rounds. Maj Aramaki, therefore, decided to send WO Umekawa off first with the practice ammunition and then follow on in another prototype after it had been re-armed with the explosive rounds.

After takeoff WO Umekawa encountered a B-25B Mitchell over Kasumigaura heading south at an altitude of about 1000 ft, and he made his first gunnery pass as the enemy aircraft crossed the coastline. Evading return fire from the bomber's gun turret, he completed a second and third pass, noting that the gunner had ceased firing. His fire had hit the bomber near the wing root and he saw oil or fuel streaming back. Umekawa wanted to continue his attack, but by that stage his fuel was low and he decided to break off and return to base, rather than risk damaging the valuable prototype in a forced landing.

Maj Aramaki took off from Mito in the other prototype once it had been re-armed, setting off in pursuit of the B-25s. However, Zero-sen fighters from the IJNAF's Yokosuka Kokutai spotted his unfamiliar fighter and prepared to attack it. The Japanese military was aware of the impending carrier strike and had called its air defences to readiness, but it was presumed that the raid would occur a day later on 19 April as the carrier would need to approach closer to the mainland to launch its fighters. Therefore, there was an expectation of encountering enemy

Although the Ki-61 prototypes tested at the Army Flight Test Centre at Fussa were flown in combat against the Doolittle raid on Tokyo in April 1942, firing their guns in anger for the first time, it would be more than a year before the type was deployed with frontline units. The first of three prototypes was completed in December 1941, and nine additional prototypes were manufactured up to July 1942 (*via Osprey Publishing*)

A trio of factory-fresh Ki-61 fighters of the Akeno Rikugun Koku Gakko (Army Flying School) in Japan, with the unit emblem applied to their rudders. This marking represents Yata No Kagami (the Sacred Mirror of Yata), one of Japan's Imperial regalia, together with a stylised representation of the first Kanji character for Akeno. The Japanese characters above the emblem represent '86', which was probably the aircraft's serial number (*Author's collection*)

fighters. As the Zero-sens came in to attack his Hien, Maj Aramaki banked sharply to display the Japanese Hinomaru (sun's red disc) on his wings and waggled them to prevent a friendly fire incident. After this encounter he could not locate any enemy bombers and returned to base without engaging.

It seems likely that WO Umekawa had in fact made attacks on two different B-25s during the raid. Lt Everett W Holstrom's B-25B (40-2282), which took off from the aircraft carrier USS *Hornet* (CV-8) at 0833 hrs, appears to have been the target of Umekawa's first gunnery run. Holstrom had already experienced problems during the mission prior to encountering any Japanese fighters, his aircraft suffering fuel leakage from the left wing tank. The B-25's mid-upper turret was also out of commission due to electrical and hydraulic failures. After some firing passes by Type 97 (Ki-27) fighters, which convinced Holstrom to jettison his bombs, his navigator, Lt Harry McCool, reported seeing several pursuits that looked like British Spitfires. Holstrom then saw one of these fighters on his right side after it had made a gunnery run on the bomber, and he later described it as having an inline engine, retractable gear and double tapered wings.

Intercepting Hiens were also reported by B-25B 40-2249 *Hari Kari-er* of Capt C Ross Greening after it had flown over Kasumigaura Lake, 20 miles southwest of Mito. Capt Greening's Mitchell was the 11th of 16 aircraft to depart *Hornet* at 0856 hrs, and it had crossed the coast north of the expected course. Greening reported that they had come under 'sustained attack' by four aircraft of unknown type, described as 'new model fighters closely resembling Zeros except for their inline engines' with six machine guns in the wings. In later years Greening confirmed the

This Ki-61-I (retro-designated Ko) is usually captioned as a Hien on a delivery flight, although it is probably one of the earliest production models on a test flight – perhaps serial number 114, manufactured in September 1942. The spinner is unpainted and there appears to be no anti-glare panel (*via Osprey Publishing*)

Another, or possibly the same, early production Hien. The vertical canopy brace was introduced from the second prototype, serial number 6102 (*San Diego Air & Space Museum*)

Akeno Hien '06'. Note that its fabric-covered rudder, elevators and ailerons are doped aluminium, rather than light grey (*via Osprey Publishing*)

identity of the aircraft as a Ki-61 from the intelligence data then available.

The B-25 mid-upper gunner was reported to have hit two of the Japanese fighters, one of which 'wobbled off' whilst a second was seen in flames. The remaining two fighters inflicted light damage on the B-25 after the gunner had run out of ammunition. The B-25's navigator, Lt Frank J Kappeler, gave a slightly different account, reporting that four fighters had 'come out of nowhere' while they were about 30 miles out from their target. One of them had made a pass at the B-25 whilst it was still flying at cruising speed (probably Umekawa's second attack on what he believed was Holstrom's B-25). After this attack Greening shoved the throttles forward and when the fighter attempted another pass (probably Umekawa's third attack) it was driven off by a few bursts from the turret gunner, Sgt Melvin J Gardner. Once speed had increased to 260 mph 'the fighters found it difficult to overtake us'.

As the B-25 approached its primary target, the crew noticed enemy aircraft converging on them from all directions. Greening then chose to attack his alternative target of an oil refinery and tank farm. Moments after the Mitchell had dropped its bombs from 600 ft instead of 1500 ft, another Japanese fighter made a pass on the B-25. Kappeler reported that Gardner scored a direct hit on this fighter, seeing it pull up into a steep climb, smoking heavily. It is apparent that this Japanese fighter was not the Ki-61 that had attacked earlier. Kappeler's account of the incident coincides with that of WO Umekawa. It appears that Greening's aircraft was the target of Umekawa's second and third gunnery runs, the warrant officer believing he was engaging the same B-25 he had attacked during his first run. This was the first combat sortie of the Ki-61 to inflict damage on an enemy aircraft.

CHAPTER TWO

RUSH TO COMBAT

fter a relatively long and troublesome gestation the Ki-61 was finally introduced into service during the early months of 1943. A deteriorating situation in New Guinea increased the urgency of re-equipping, and in mid-1943 two Hiko Sentai (Air or Flying Regiments – in usage, the word 'Hiko' for air or flying is often dropped), the 68th and 78th, were hurried to that theatre with their new Ki-61 fighters. Despite increasing logistical and maintenance difficulties, the effectiveness of the Ki-61 in air combat, in a theatre where the relatively modestly armed Ki-43 constituted the main strength of the IJAAF's fighter force, was largely proven and a number of pilots would add to their existing scores or become aces on the type. These included Susumu Kajinami, Hiroshi Sekiguchi, Takashi Noguchi, Shogo Takeuchi and Mitsuyoshi Tarui of the 68th, and Mitsusada Asai, Chuichi Ichikawa, Tokuyasu Ishizuka, Shogo Saito, Keiji Takamiya and Takashi Tomishima of the 78th.

The 68th and 78th Sentais had been formed as part of an IJAAF response to the German attack on the Soviet Union in June 1941, Japan's military leadership envisaging a rapid reinforcement and build-up of air assets in Manchuria for potential war with the USSR. Towards the end of the year, and in the face of increasing operational demands elsewhere, the original offensive plan 'A' for the IJAAF to initiate operations against the Soviet Union was modified by Lt Gen Ritsudo Suzuki, the commander of the Kwangtung Army Air Unit, which was to become the 2nd Kokugun (Air

The 68th Sentai poses for a group photo at Akeno before flying south into the maelstrom of New Guinea. Few of these men would ever return home (*Yasuho Izawa*)

Army) in May 1942. A new plan 'B' for the IJAAF to initiate offensive operations only in response to a Soviet attack, together with a major efficiency drive for the air assets stationed in Manchuria, facilitated the transfer of units to more active theatres.

By the end of 1942 the 68th and 78th were brigaded together within the 14th Hikodan (Air Brigade) under the command of Col Tateyama, and were scheduled to sequentially convert to the Ki-61 in Japan, before being transferred from the 4th Hikoshidan (Air Division) of the 2nd Kokugun to the 6th Hikoshidan of the 4th Kokugun, headquartered at Rabaul, on New Britain.

The 68th Sentai was originally formed at Harbin, in Manchuria, in March 1942 from elements of the 9th, 13th and 64th Sentais. It was initially equipped with the Ki-27 fighter (see Aircraft of the Aces 103), and from December 1942 began type transition to the Ki-61 at the Akeno Rikugun Koku Gakko (Army Aviation School) in Japan. The 68th was the first operational unit to do so, and at a time when only 34 production examples of the new fighter were available. The unit was commanded by Maj Noboru Shimoyama during the transition.

The 78th Sentai had also been formed in March 1942 from elements of the 24th and 33rd Hiko Sentais at Hsingshu (Xingshu), in eastern Manchuria, and was also equipped with the Ki-27 fighter. Although an original intention to re-equip the 78th with the Ki-43 fighter (see *Aircraft of the Aces 85*) saw small numbers of that type reportedly issued to the unit when it was stationed at Sunjia, near Harbin, from April to December 1942, the unit subsequently transitioned to the Ki-61 at Akeno from April 1943 whilst under the command of Maj Akira Takatsuki.

One of the pilots assigned to the 68th who would become a Hien ace over New Guinea was Sgt Susumu Kajinami, born in 1923 in Osaka Prefecture as an only son. At that time the Hanshin Flying School operated from Yao airfield near his home. He visited the school many times and was able to closely examine a Type 91 fighter. At his junior high school Kajinami applied to join the IJAAF without telling his parents. His application was approved, but at that time flying was thought to be a very dangerous occupation and most of his neighbours could not understand his decision.

Sgt Sasumu Kajinami of the 68th Sentai poses with camouflaged Hien serial number 388, which was assigned to him at Kagamigahara in July 1943. He was one of the lucky ones who returned to Japan, surviving the war as a 24-victory ace (*via Osprey Publishing*)

Following graduation Kajinami entered the Tachikawa Flying School, and the following year the Kumagaya flying school to undertake bomber crew training. There, he switched to fighter pilot training and graduated in December 1941, four months earlier than was normal, just as the Pacific War broke out.

Kajinami was assigned to the Ki-27-equipped 246th Sentai at Kakogawa, where he flew in the 2nd Chutai (squadron) under the command of Akira Okada, from whom he received additional one-on-one training. Some four months later he was assigned to the 68th Sentai and proceeded to Akeno, where he received further training on the Ki-27 and Ki-43 for a month, before starting to fly Ki-61 Hien serial number 103, the first production aircraft to be assigned to the unit. Most pilots in Kajinami's unit called the Ki-61 simply 'roku-ichi' ('six-one'), rather than 'Hien' or 'Ki-61'.

In July 1943 Kajinami was assigned Ki-61 Ko serial number 388 at Kagamigahara airfield, where it was camouflaged with dark green paint and had a white band – the senchi hiyoshiki (war front) marking – painted around the rear fuselage. Several days before his departure to New Guinea his mother came to visit him at the airfield, and they shared lunch together under the wing of the Hien. His mother entreated him to have luck and to survive, caressing the fuselage of his Hien with her blessing – a memorably emotive moment for both of them.

ENGINE WOES

The Hien was the most formidable IJAAF fighter deployed in New Guinea but it was to suffer from technical shortcomings in its engine configuration that were exacerbated by conditions in the field and the challenges of adequate maintenance. The very high pressure of the Mitsubishi fuel injection system led to fuel leakage and fuel line ruptures. The ignition system was troublesome, with poor quality spark plugs causing pre-ignition or constant fouling. Leaks in the coolant system due to poor castings caused overheating and the quality of bearings caused many failures. Cumulatively, these issues militated against the effectiveness of the design as a combat fighter, and prevented it from reaching its potential in the most crucial aerial campaigns facing the IJAAF. They also led to a lack of confidence in the fighter by those pilots flying it in combat for the first time, and who were familiar with the more reliable radial, air-cooled engines fitted in all other IJAAF types.

In New Guinea there were ongoing problems with insufficient numbers of mechanics and inadequate maintenance facilities, and this, combined with the number of aircraft available, ultimately proved crippling. Maj Yasuhiko Kuroe, a leading IJAAF ace and test pilot (see *Aircraft of the Aces 13, 85, 100* and *103* for further details) recalled the Hien as follows;

'When I was at the Army Flight Test Centre in Fussa, I saw the Hien for the first time and was impressed by its graceful form. Its performance was in general "good", but the problem seems to be due to Ha 40 V-shaped engine (1175 hp), which was license-built in Japan. Of course the Japanese Army had little experience with liquid-cooled engines, and most of the maintenance crews had no expertise with this type of engine. From flying the Hien in many tests I felt that a slightly more powerful engine would best fit with the airframe and make the Hien a more powerful fighter.'

THE NUMBERS GAME

Any consideration of the impact and effectiveness of the Hien units on the New Guinea air campaign must take into account the relative numbers of aircraft deployed. The two Hien Sentai of the 14th Hikodan should have deployed with a combined strength of about 112 aircraft – the equivalent of nine RAF squadrons. There were usually more pilots than available aircraft, so for example at the end of May 1943 the 68th had 41 pilots, of whom 15 were officers, but only 18 serviceable fighters. Seven more required first-line maintenance or repair and one was in need of major repair, with each Chutai effectively operating at half strength.

The net result of these low numbers was that the more experienced pilots would fly most often on operations, putting themselves at greater risk and bearing the brunt of combat stress, whilst the newer or more junior pilots had less opportunity to gain the experience necessary to survive in combat. For example, in one Chutai (squadron) in New Guinea the unit's leading ace flew more than 90 hours in a month, whilst two of its 'ordinary' pilots accrued only 11 and 17 hours, respectively. With attrition, this imbalance created a spiral of decline in capability that effectively prevented the Hien pilots gaining parity, let alone the upper hand in the campaign, even though in individual encounters the aircraft was to remain a formidable foe.

By the end of June 1943 the 68th had only 20 serviceable aircraft, with six requiring first-line maintenance or repair. From August 1943 to April 1944 the available serviceable strength of the 68th averaged only seven Hiens a day – less than half a single Chutai (the latter usually had 18 aircraft when at full strength), and just over 12 percent of the authorised Sentai strength. The 68th had to augment its sorties with the Ki-43, which on several occasions exceeded the number of Hiens available. The 78th Sentai fared little better, averaging only eight serviceable Hiens per day over the same period, and it was also forced to operate the 'Oscar' alongside the Kawasaki fighter. Consequently, sorties were often flown by both units in combination, but even together the two Sentais were seldom able to field the official strength of a single Sentai.

Throughout their deployment in New Guinea both Sentais had to send parties of pilots to the IJAAF air depot in Manila, in the Philippines, to collect new aircraft ferried in from Japan or repaired fighters ready for service again, as well as to lead replacement pilots to the frontline. This denuded the units in the war zone of experienced pilots, often at critical times, and was another reason why the Hien failed to make a strategic impact in-theatre.

At the commencement of Hien operations over New Guinea the USAAF's Fifth Air Force fighter opposition consisted of three fighter groups, the 8th, 35th and 49th, each with three fighter squadrons, one of which was equipped with the P-38 Lightning. The 348th FG joined operations with the P-47 Thunderbolt in June 1943, the 475th FG with P-38 Lightnings in mid-July 1943 and the 58th FG, also with the P-47, at the end of the year, bringing the number of US fighter squadrons in-theatre to 18. By the beginning of 1944 four squadrons were flying the P-38 and no fewer than 11 squadrons were equipped with the P-47. In addition to the USAAF presence, the Kittyhawk-equipped Nos 75, 76 and

The 3rd Chutai of the 78th Sentai photographed at Akeno before going to New Guinea. Seated fourth from left is the 3rd Chutai leader Capt Ryoichi Tateyama, who would subsequently lead both depleted Sentais from 9 March 1944 (*Yasuho Izawa*)

77 Sqns of the Royal Australian Air Force (RAAF) engaged in close support and air defence duties, while No 79 Sqn RAAF, equipped with the Spitfire VC, operated from Milne Bay, Goodenough Island and later Kiriwina, off the eastern tip of New Guinea. In early 1944 RAAF operations over eastern New Guinea were augmented by the arrival of Nos 80 and 82 Sqns, equipped with the P-40N.

DISASTROUS FERRY FLIGHT

The first elements of the 68th Sentai to be sent to New Guinea flew to Yokosuka in early April 1943 and then travelled to Truk as deck cargo onboard the escort carrier *Taiyō*, arriving on 10 April. To avoid the danger posed by Allied submarines in the South Pacific, the aircraft were required to fly on to Rabaul. IJAAF fighter pilots were not well trained in long haul over water navigation, and in the first attempt to make this 745-mile journey on 25 April they had to turn back due to bad weather. The aircraft flown by Sgt Maj Shoichi Ohki was lost.

The second attempt was made two days later on 27 April with two groups of 13 and 14 aircraft each, led by a twin-engined Mitsubishi Ki-46 'Dinah' reconnaissance aeroplane as a pathfinder to provide navigation. The first group got into trouble when a number of aircraft fell behind due to engine problems and the Ki-46 turned back to find them. The remaining Ki-61 pilots soon became lost, with compass faults, electrical issues and engine failures adding to their woes. Two pilots turned back to Truk, another managed to find his way to Kavieng and landed there safely, but eight others had to ditch in deep water off Nuguria Atoll nearly 200 miles north of Rabaul. There, seven of the pilots were reportedly attacked and murdered by the islanders, with only one surviving. The remaining two Hiens were never seen again.

The second group of 14 Ki-61s were led to a safe landing at Vunakanau airfield, Rabaul, by their Ki-46 pathfinder, where they attracted the curiosity of the personnel of the 751st Kokutai – an IJNAF bomber unit flying the Mitsubishi G4M 'Betty' bomber. CPO Kunishige Kuwaori, a pilot in the 751st, saw the new IJAAF fighters arrive but was forbidden from taking a closer look. He did not know who had flown them in. A second ferry flight from Truk to Rabaul on 3 May ran into bad weather and was forced to turn back also losing aircraft in the process.

As a result of the ferrying disasters the remaining elements of the 68th and later the 78th would take the notionally safer, but longer, route to New Guinea via Okinawa, Taiwan, the Philippines, Mindanao and the Celebes to Western New Guinea – a 5500-mile journey that exacerbated the problems of reinforcement and supply to the air units operating in

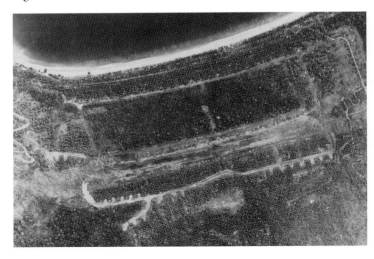

Boram airfield on the north coast of New Guinea, also known as Wewak East, would be home to the 68th and 78th Sentais when they took the Hien into combat. The Japanese were hindered in airfield construction by their lack of heavy earth-moving equipment, being forced to rely on manpower alone. This in turn limited the extent of their dispersal facilities (*US National Archive*)

New Guinea. Staging via the Philippines to Rabaul in June, the 78th still lost 12 of its 45 fighters. From July the Hien units began staging from Rabaul to Wewak, on the north coast of New Guinea, in preparation for commencing sorties over the Salamaua area, but even those flights were not without mishap and aircraft were lost en route due to weather conditions, navigational errors or mechanical failures.

At Wewak the IJAAF units were concentrated on four airfield complexes – Wewak main, Dagua, But (also known as Dagua East) and Boram (also known as Wewak East). The 68th and 78th took up residence at Boram, where they joined the Kawasaki Ki-45 Toryu 'Nick' twin-engined heavy fighters of the 13th Sentai's 2nd and 3rd Chutais.

On 20 September 1943 Sgt Kajinami took off from Kagamigahara in the Hien serial number 388 blessed by his mother to fly the longer staging route to Wewak via Heito in southwestern Taiwan (sometimes referred to as Peito and now called Pingtung), Clark Field in the Philippines, Davao on Mindanao, Medona in the Celebes and, finally, Solon in Western New Guinea. Shortly after his arrival at Wewak there was an air raid alert and Kajinami took shelter whilst another duty pilot scrambled in his 388. Four days after his arrival he was allocated 436, a newer Hien, but one that had been damaged in air combat two days previously and already sported 20 duralumin patches. Sgt Kajinami subsequently flew in combat over New Guinea as a member of the 2nd Chutai for about seven months.

Sgt Kajinami considered the Ki-27 to be more like a sports aircraft with its agility, but he did not like the Ki-43 due to its weak structure. He preferred the Hien for its much tougher structure, considering that to be one of the main reasons he survived combat over New Guinea. In contrast to the opinion of other IJAAF pilots, he thought the DB 601 engine was very robust, and after one encounter it got him home safely despite having suffered damage from two hits. During dogfights the Hien could attain 328 mph without sustaining damage to the airframe, whereas the 'Oscar' would often suffer structural failures if flown at high speed and subjected to violent manouevring.

The fuel injection pump fitted to the Hien was problematic, however, and without adequate maintenance it often failed, causing the engine to stop abruptly. There was also an intermittent problem with the propeller whereby the pitch control sometimes jammed, preventing the aircraft from being able to climb properly. Another significant weakness of the Hien was the auxiliary fuel tank in the fuselage. Not only could it explode suddenly if hit, the tank also made the aircraft tail heavy and caused it to pitch up when fully loaded. This meant that the Hien was prone to stalling during takeoffs and landings, resulting in the deaths of many pilots. The dangers posed by this tank were such that the 68th Sentai commander Maj Noburo Shimoyama ordered its removal from the aircraft flown by his unit. This move was not universal, however, as members of the 244th Sentai in Japan recall that the fuselage tank remained installed, but it was not used for combat missions. There are also several photographs of 244th Hiens having their auxiliary tanks filled and fuel staining the fuselages of the aircraft.

Sgt Kajinami's description of the Hien's characteristics was reflected by USAAF pilots in New Guinea, who reported that in a shallow dive at various altitudes from 18,000 ft down to low level the 'Tony' could match the P-38 at an indicated airspeed of 400 mph. This was much faster than any other IJAAF or IJNAF fighter encountered in-theatre. When the US Navy tested a captured Hien Otsu it was less impressed, however, rating it slower in speed and rate of climb than the Hellcat and Corsair, but not the Wildcat. They also confirmed the technical issues that plagued the 'Tony' in New Guinea, noting that a great deal of maintenance was required to keep it flying. The compact engine installation made servicing and repair difficult to perform and the hydraulics were problematic. In addition, pressure system malfunctions compromised altitude performance and the propeller and supercharger controls were unsatisfactory. Optimum performance was reported to be achieved at 14,000 ft.

The Hien's guns sometimes jammed with continuous firing but Sgt Kajinami never experienced them exploding, which occasionally happened with the 'Oscar'. The Japanese-manufactured guns used oil pressure to clear jams, but the German Mauser cannon in the Hei were electrical, and a jam could be cleared very quickly in about a second (see Appendix 1). The relatively long nose of the Hien made taxiing on the ground rather difficult and the aircraft had to be taxied in a slow meandering zig-zag to reach the runaway, with the pilot standing up in the cockpit to be able to see forward. Sgt Kajinami praised the Hien for its undercarriage, which was more robust and reliable than the 'Oscar', with its wide track preventing ground loops – he had never heard of the undercarriage failing.

The installation of the armour panels to protect the pilot's head and back was also appreciated, although the Hien did not have an armoured windscreen. Its cockpit was quite spacious, with ease of entry 'like a bathtub' in contrast to the 'Oscar', which Sgt Kajinami had often experienced difficulty climbing into and sometimes hurt his shoulders on the cockpit rim once seated.

HIEN IN COMBAT

The first clash between Hien units and the enemy occurred during an escort mission to attack Salamaua on 18 July 1943 when P-38s of the 39th FS/35th FG were engaged over the target while covering USAAF transports returning from Marilinan. A 78th Sentai Hien Shotai (flight of four) came down on the Lightnings as they in turn dived after the rest of the IJAAF formation from 20,000 ft, but the brief fight was inconsequential. A P-38 was claimed by 1Lt Takashi Tomishima, although none were actually lost. Lt L P Shipley fired at what he believed was an 'Me 109' as it dived across his nose.

Two days later Capt Shogo Takeuchi's 2nd Chutai of the 68th triumphantly claimed the first victory for the unit when it downed a Liberator over Bena Bena. This was B-24D 42-40327 *Virgin III* of the 320th BS/90th BG, flown by 1Lt J B Willcoxon, that was returning to 5 Mile Drome at Port Moresby following a lone bombing mission on Madang. The B-24 exploded in midair and crashed after being attacked by the Hiens, with only one of

Gun camera film of a 'Tony' over New Guinea. When the fighter was first encountered by American pilots they believed it to be a derivative of the German Bf 109 (*via Osprey Publishing*)

Shogo Takeuchi, leading ace of the 68th Sentai, poses for a photograph in the cockpit of an 'Oscar' whilst serving with the 64th Sentai. He was a tenacious flyer, and after being wounded in a dogfight in October 1943 he returned to combat still wearing bandages. Takeuchi was killed on 21 December 1943 trying to land his battle-damaged Hien at Hansa Bay (*Yasuho Izawa*)

the gunners surviving. Takeuchi was an accomplished 25-year-old veteran of the 64th Sentai who, as a lieutenant, had fought over Malaya, the Netherlands East Indies and Burma, claiming a trio of Hurricanes destroyed over Singapore on 31 January 1942. His final tally would number 19 destroyed and 11 damaged (see *Aircraft of the Aces 85*). Over New Guinea he would claim a further 16 destroyed and ten probables, reportedly adorning the fuselage of his Hien with 58 red 'victory' eagle's wings. In the West, Shogo Takeuchi is one of the best known of the Hien aces over New Guinea.

IJAAF victory markings were usually painted solid or transfixed by an arrow to indicate a confirmed victory, but in outline only for a probable or damaged. There was no standard symbol, with various stylised eagles, bird wings, aircraft silhouettes, shooting stars and even Hinomaru flags all being used. It was also the practice in some Sentai for all members of a Shotai or 'rotte' (a fighting pair – two rotte made up a Shotai of four) to share the victories and to paint the combined tally on each aircraft, but some units frowned on the display of victory tallies and considered it unseemly boasting by individuals. Confirmation criteria were also a matter for individual Sentai, and there were no standardised rules for recording or verifying claims.

On 21 July the P-38 pilots got a better look at the 'Tony' when the 68th and 78th Sentais again clashed with the 39th FS, this time accompanied by Lightnings from the 80th FS/8th FG. The two Hien units had sortied 20 fighters to escort Ki-48 'Lily' light bombers of the 208th Sentai in a raid against an Allied beachhead in Nassau Bay. They were accompanied by an equal number of 'Oscars' from the 1st and 24th Sentais. The P-38s were at 14,000 ft escorting a force of B-25s sent to bomb Bogadjim, about 17 miles south of Madang on the north coast of New Guinea. They had just arrived over the target when they ran into the Japanese force, which was still about 150 miles from its own objective. The P-38 pilots bored straight into the 'Oscar' escorts, which they identified as Zeros, and as the formations broke into battle the Hiens dropped down from their position as top cover and hit the USAAF fighters hard.

The 78th was subsequently credited with five Lightnings destroyed, with the newly arrived 22-year-old 1Lt Keiji Takamiya of the 2nd Chutai claiming his first kill despite having no previous combat experience. A natural fighter pilot, Takamiya went on to claim 17 victories in six months over New Guinea to become one of only two recognised 78th Sentai aces. Three Lightnings were claimed by the 2nd Chutai leader 1Lt Takashi Tomishima, who was in turn seriously wounded in the arm during the fight and hospitalised thereafter. The P-38 pilots claimed 11 destroyed and four probables, with two 'Tonys' claimed by Lt R E Smith and one by Lt S O Andrews (who identified his opponent as an 'Me 109'), making them both aces. Andrews' gun camera film provided the first clear evidence of the presence of the Kawasaki fighter over New Guinea. The 78th lost 1Lts Kuniji Fujita and Kuruhiko Suzuki, and several other pilots were reported missing following forced landings.

Two days later the Hiens and Lightnings clashed near Bogadjim again. WO Tokuyasu Ishizuka was leading a mixed flight from the 68th and 78th Sentais on a patrol, together with 15 'Oscars' from the 24th Sentai, when they ran into Lightnings from the 39th and 80th FSs that were escorting both transport aircraft and B-24s. The IJAAF fighters went into a 'Lufberry circle' in scissoring flights of four as the 39th FS flew through them, although Ishizuka led his Shotai up in a steep climb in an attempt to get above the P-38s. The Shotai was then hit from above by the 80th FS as it climbed, resulting in Sgt Maj Hideji Sekiya of the 68th Sentai and 1Lt Hiroshi Suemitsu of the 78th Sentai being shot down.

Ishizuka claimed three P-38s destroyed and the 'Oscars' seven, but only the P-38 of Capt C Jones of the 80th FS was actually lost. Jones had a hung-up drop tank, which was set on fire during the combat, and he crashed during an attempted forced landing. The P-38 of Maj C W King of the 39th FS was also hit, but it returned damaged with an engine fire that had destroyed the port boom and resulted in the fighter being written off. The 80th FS claimed six 'Oscars' and one 'Tony' destroyed, with another 'Tony' as a probable. The 39th FS claimed five victories, with one Tony as a probable.

The American pilots reported that the Ki-61 was fast – faster than the Zero and 'Oscar' – and could not be caught or outrun in a shallow dive from 18,000 ft at 400 mph indicated air speed.

By the end of July the serviceable strength of both Sentais combined was only 23 aircraft. Then on 17 and 18 August 1943 two devastating Allied air attacks against the Japanese airfields at Wewak left the 68th with only six Hiens and the 78th with none. Both units had to withdraw to Manila to re-equip with new fighters, the 78th returning to Wewak at the end of the month and the 68th at the beginning of September. Capt Takeuchi's 2nd Chutai of the 68th was deployed to Cape Gloucester (Tuvulu) on the northwest tip of New Britain to provide convoy patrols to counter increasing RAAF Beaufighter strikes against barge traffic in the surrounding coastal areas.

The red-trimmed Hiens of Takeuchi's New Britain detachment may have ventured even further afield because on 3 September, whilst escorting B-24s to bomb Kahili (Buin), on Bougainville, with seven other Kittyhawks, Flt Sgt N A Pirie of No 16 Sqn Royal New Zealand Air Force (RNZAF) reported being attacked by a single 'Tony' in a hit-and-run pass. Both wings of his Kittyhawk were hit and shrapnel damaged the cockpit. Pirie's engine seized, but he was able to glide the fighter down to a safe ditching on a reef at Vella Lavella.

On 11 September Takeuchi reportedly shot down RAAF Seagull V A2-19 of No 1 RCS, the amphibian being crewed by Flg Offs R G Bonython (pilot) and R A Kelley (navigator) of No 30 Sqn. The aeroplane was searching for the crew of a No 30 Sqn Beaufighter that had ditched off the south coast of New Britain two days earlier. A covering force of F4Us for a bombing raid against Kahili (Buin) also reported encountering 'Tonys' between Shortland and Fauro islands on the 11th, the Corsair pilots claiming two destroyed – there were no corresponding 68th Sentai fatalities, however.

68th Sentai Hiens photographed at Boram during a low-level Allied air raid on 16 October 1943. The Hien on the left has been cannibalised for spare parts – the latter were always in short supply in New Guinea. The Ki-61 to the right features the 68th Sentai's early tail marking, which appears to have been obscured with camouflage of some sort (*via Darryl Ford*)

The following day Takeuchi claimed a Boston III downed over Gasmata during an Allied raid on the airfield. This was possibly A28-15 of No 22 Sqn RAAF, flown by Flt Lt H B Dawkins, which failed to return, although the Squadron ORB attributes the loss to anti-aircraft fire and recorded that the aircraft ditched in the sea 35 miles south of the enemy airfield.

A component of the 78th withdrew again to Manila on 19 September to replenish its aircraft strength, eventually returning to New Guinea on 20 October with 20 Hiens. By the end of September 1943 the 68th at Wewak was back down to two aircraft, and on 2 October it began flying ten Ki-43s left in New Guinea by the 24th Sentai.

At the end of September Sgt Kajinami claimed his first victory. He was flying as wingman to MSgt Matsui in a Shotai patrol led by 1Lt Inoue over Wewak when four P-40s were engaged. With the support of Matsui, he downed one of the Curtiss fighters.

On 16 October the 68th and 78th clashed with the enemy in three separate combats, the Hiens and 'Oscars' bouncing a force of P-47s from the 340th FS/348th FG that were escorting two flights of B-25s sent to bomb Alexishafen. Although the Japanese had an altitude advantage of 1000 ft, the Thunderbolt pilots managed to turn into them and claim two 'Tonys' and several 'Oscars' destroyed for no loss. P-38 pilots from the 8th FG's 80th FS also claimed four 'Tonys' over Boram. That same day Sgt Maj Jukichi Fujii of the 68th Sentai claimed three P-47s destroyed, only to be shot down and wounded over Madang by P-38s of the 49th FG's 9th FS on a sweep a few hours later. He was probably flying an 'Oscar' because his victor, 2Lt G Haniotis, claimed a lone 'Zeke' (Mitsubishi A6M Zero).

Although the nature of these combats precludes attributing the losses accurately, the 68th had Sgt Kiyoshi Ito killed. The 78th lost three pilots, namely the 1st Chutai leader Capt Yoshichika Mutaguchi and experienced NCOs WO Shiro Nonaka and Sgt Maj Fujio Tanogami. There must have been more bail outs or fighters returning that were severely damaged because of the 17 aircraft (including five 'Oscars') available to the 68th before the combat, only nine (including three Oscars) were serviceable the following day. The 78th was in even worse shape, being reduced to just four airworthy Hiens.

On 22 October the P-47Ds of the 348th FG were well and truly bounced by the two Sentais during a low-level escort mission of B-25s to

Wewak. The 342nd FS was the lead squadron, with eight P-47s at 2000 ft, when its rear flight was engaged by seven 'Tonys' led by CO Maj Kiyoshi Kimura's 68th Sentai Hombu (HQ) flight. Although Lt W Frankfort bailed out and managed to walk back to base Lt E R Ness (in 42-8145) was last seen with a 'Tony' on his tail and failed to return. The lead Thunderbolt flight turned back into the attack and future ace Capt W G Benz fired at a Ki-61 pursuing a P-47, then dived after another going for the

Hiens of the 68th Sentai detachment at Vunakanau airfield, on New Britain, in October 1943. The 'Tony' in the foreground has the broad fuselage band of a Chutai commander, apparently applied in white (*via Darryl Ford*)

B-25s and shot it down in flames into the sea. Two more 'Tonys' that had possibly zoom-climbed back up above the P-47s then dived on the two 342nd FS flights and Benz claimed one of them as it turned to intervene against a Thunderbolt that had latched onto the tail of his comrade.

The 341st FS was flying at 5000 ft when it was bounced by five 'Tonys' that dived on the P-47s from behind a cloud. Lt H Jacoby (in 42-8117) was shot down and failed to return. The P-47s claimed two 'Tonys' and one 'Oscar' destroyed and one 'Tony' probable (the 68th Sentai was flying a mixed complement of Ki-61s and Ki-43s). 1Lt Ryuzo Tsujii and Sgt Shigeru Chiba of the 68th Sentai were killed in action. The Hien pilots in turn had shot down three P-47s. It is possible that Sgt Maj Fujii died from previous wounds on this day, or had flown again despite his wounds and was downed during the encounter with the 348th, receiving a posthumous promotion, for a Lt Fujii was reported killed on 22 October.

Two day later, in misty conditions of low cloud, Takeuchi was flying alone in an attempted interception of B-25 strafers from the 3rd BG that were attacking Rabaul's Tobera airfield when he was caught by two Lightnings of the 49th FG's 9th FS. Future ace Lt R H Wandrey pulled in behind Takeuchi's Hien and fired a burst that appeared to hit its engine – pieces came away from the Ki-61 and a plume of oil spattered the P-38's windscreen. Takeuchi rolled over and escaped in a steep dive, having been wounded in the attack. He was hospitalised, but after two weeks, frustrated by inactivity and defying medical advice, he insisted on returning to combat operations, still bandaged and with unhealed wounds.

In New Guinea the hit-and-run 'rotte' tactics increasingly adopted by the Hien pilots were known as Ganryu-jima in reference to the site of a famous duel between the Samurai warriors Musashi Miyamoto and Kojiro Sasaki. In that fight the famed swordsman Miyamoto killed Sasaki with one sword blow and then fled from the island before the arrival of Sasaki's vengeful comrades. In practice the transitional IJAAF doctrine from turning battle to vertical combat was conflicted, and all too often the Hien pilots failed to dive away after an initial aggressive bounce from a superior position and allowed themselves to become engaged piecemeal with the enemy in uncoordinated manoeuvres, ultimately suffering losses from the superior numbers ranged against them.

Inexperienced pilots finding themselves isolated in battle were shot down or, in some cases, fled, became lost and were forced to crash land or bail out miles from their airfields. In one incident a lone Hien pilot flying aimlessly at low level over the New Guinea highlands was shot down by fire from Australian ground troops mystified by the sudden appearance and behaviour of the Japanese fighter.

Sgt Kajinami described a Wewak air defence sortie during the autumn of 1943 when he was flying as wingman to the acting Chutai leader, 1Lt Nakagawa. Their formation of eight Hiens was flying eastward at just under 20,000 ft to intercept a force of about 80 enemy aircraft consisting of bombers escorted by fighters. On seeing the enemy formation, they made a right hand climbing turn, but the enemy fighters had also seen them and dropped their auxiliary tanks to climb. The Hiens then ran into a large formation of P-40s and turned to the left to get onto their tails.

'At that moment a stream of tracers crossed in front of me and I flung the six-one into a steep turning climb to evade the attacker', Kajinami recalled. 'As the turn tightened the aircraft suddenly stalled, falling down below the fight, and I found myself alone in the air. Two P-47s then appeared above me and dived at me head on, but I passed underneath them, evading their fire, and didn't see them again.'

Kajinami then climbed to 20,000 ft and saw the dogfight still in progress below him at about 5000 ft. As he approached the fight he recognised 1Lt Inoue being pursued by four P-40s, so he went into a steep dive to catch them and fired a burst of 12.7 mm ammunition at the rearmost P-40 from a range of about 100 yards. Although the enemy fighter began to burn and then fell away, the other P-40 pilots appeared not to notice Kajinami's attack and continued their pursuit of Inoue. He then dived below the P-40s, climbing sharply to fire at, and hit, the last one, which appeared to explode in midair. The two remaining P-40s then pulled away in a tight diving turn.

During this engagement Kajinami also claimed a P-47 destroyed for a total of three kills, but he then came under attack from a second Thunderbolt. His Hien was hit 29 times, wounding him in the left leg and burning his right arm. Without the armour plate, which stopped one round near his head and five at his back, and if the fuselage fuel tank had not been removed from the aircraft, Sgt Kajinami believed he would not have survived that encounter. He considered the P-47 to be the most formidable of the Hien's opponents.

At the end of October the bulk of the 68th withdrew to Manila to rest and replenish again, leaving the 78th to continue the fight alone with a mixed compliment of Hiens and 'Oscars' that never exceeded 17 operational aircraft in total, or more than 12 serviceable Hiens at any one

Two cannibalised Hiens in the dump at Vunakanau reveal command markings. The 68th Sentai Hien on the left has a slanting fuselage stripe associated with a Shotai leader, whilst the one on the right has the broader vertical stripe of a Chutai leader just forward of the fuselage roundel (via Darryl Ford)

time. The 68th's 2nd Chutai remained at Rabaul and participated in air defence sorties when US Navy carrier task forces attacked in early November. On 11 November future Corsair ace Tom Blackburn of VF-17 narrowly escaped the attention of a formation of IJAAF fighters. Having unsuccessfully pursued a Zero-sen down to 2500 ft, he had emerged alone from cloud to find six 'Tonys'

Propeller trouble! This 78th Sentai Hien was caught in the open at Boram in October 1943, hastily abandoned by the mechanics who had recently removed its spinner. The pitch control mechanism for the Ki-61's propeller was problematic throughout the fighter's brief career (*via Darryl Ford*)

at his 'four o'clock' position and 5000 ft higher, with their leader peeling down towards him. Fortunately, there was plenty of cloud about, and Blackburn was able to escape his predicament by ducking into another one, shaken by the close escape. He subsequently engaged one of the Ki-61s and claimed it shot down for the fourth of his 11 victories.

In late November Sgt Kajinami claimed a P-38 for his fifth victory during an engagement in support of Ki-48 'Lily' bombers attacking a USAAF airfield in the Markham valley. On 30 November the 1st and 3rd Chutais of the 68th returned to New Guinea with 26 Hiens on charge. Just after 1100 hrs on 1 December, Japanese gun emplacements at Boram were the target for a two-pronged attack by B-24 squadrons of the 90th BG. The 321st BS had just come off the target when a lone Hien flown by 25-year-old 2Lt Shogo Saito (a 25-victory Nomonhan veteran and ace – see Aircraft of the Aces 103 for further details) of the 78th Sentai sliced head on into the bomber formation from a 'two o'clock low' position.

Saito's near head-on attack was initially against the lead Liberator of the formation, although he skidded his Hien at the last minute to fire a devastating burst at B-24D 42-72806 *Ten Knights in a Bar Room* flown by 1Lt O Sheehan in the No 6 position, setting the No 2 engine on fire before rolling over and diving away. The B-24 was fatally damaged from Saito's single pass, and with fire blazing from the bomb-bay and fuselage, dropped out of formation and broke up as the left wing and rear fuselage buckled. Although Saito continued to fly and fight with the 78th over New Guinea after this incident, details of any further claims are unknown.

In early December elements of the 68th and 78th Sentais staged from Wewak to Madang in an attempt to secure air superiority over the US airfields at Gusap and Nadzab in the Ramu valley. On 10 December they sortied in stages for an early morning strafing and bombing raid against Gusap together with 'Oscars' from the 24th, 33rd, 63rd and 248th Sentais for a combined force of more than 80 fighters. Takeuchi's Shotai of 68th Sentai Ki-61s was able to bounce an element of four P-40Ns from the 49th FG's 8th FS led by Lt C Lambert that had been on patrol and was attempting to stalk another Japanese formation. Having initially damaged Lt W Linder's fighter, the IJAAF pilots pursued the P-40 until it force-landed in the Kunai grass below. Linder escaped with an ankle wounded by shrapnel from an exploding bullet, his P-40 having received more than 100 hits.

Meanwhile, two more flights of 68th Sentai 'Tonys' flying at 5000 ft were bounced from 9500 ft by four P-47s of the 49th FG's 9th FS, led by ace Maj G R Johnson, which had been returning to Gusap after a mission.

Former Nomonhan ace 2Lt Shogo Saito of the 78th Sentai added an unknown number of victories to his score over New Guinea flying the Ki-61, including a B-24 with a single head-on pass (*Yasuho Izawa*)

A Ki-61 was damaged by Johnson and a second example 'flamed' by Capt W Markey in the initial pass, and as the Japanese formation broke up the two P-47 pilots climbed away, turned back in and hit two more to claim three destroyed in total (the Ki-61 was Johnson's tenth of 22 victories). Although one of the 'Tony' pilots managed to bail out, he was captured and executed by Australian troops.

The action for the day was not yet over, however, as a formation of Ki-61s returning to Madang was bounced by one of two more flights of P-40s from the 49th's 8th FS that were heading back to Gusap following a sweep over Hansa Bay. The Warhawk pilots claimed two 'Tonys' in their initial pass, while a third Ki-61 pilot who was then pursuing Capt S Brinson bailed out from his apparently undamaged aircraft when Lt R M DeHaven fired a deflection shot in an attempt to distract him. This unusual success gave DeHaven ace status.

The tables were then turned on him by a skilled Hien pilot who slipped in behind DeHaven's P-40 as he attempted to dive away. Hitting the Warhawk hard, he then pursued the USAAF pilot in a tight diving spiral down to treetop height, continuing to inflict damage as the two machines lost altitude. The Hien pilot finally gave up pursuit as DeHaven pulled out and fled at low level, narrowly surviving the encounter to belly-land his fatally damaged P-40N at Gusap. The IJAAF pilot involved in this action has been identified as Shogo Takeuchi, although this cannot be confirmed from the known facts. At that time there were of course other skilled pilots in both Sentais.

The 49th claimed six 'Tonys' destroyed, although the 68th Sentai only recorded the deaths of three pilots, WO Hajimi Hazama and Sgts Masuichi Fujimoto and Tadashi Shibakiyo. The identity of the Ki-61 pilot who bailed out after being hit by Johnson is unknown. The 78th Sentai had one or two pilots wounded and one possible fatality, although the exact details remain uncertain.

By mid-December the 68th at Wewak had been reduced to just nine aircraft, and it was unable to provide an escort for bombers attacking Arawe because of the loss of personnel. The 78th had been reduced to just seven Hiens. In effect both Sentais were able to sortie little more than a single Chutai in the face of increasing numbers of P-38s and P-47s. The gloom was somewhat alleviated by the arrival of the first six Ki-61-I Hei fighters equipped with the formidable German Mauser MG 151/20 20 mm cannon in the wings (see Appendix I). These were allocated to the best pilots in the 68th and 78th, including Shogo Saito and Hiroshi Sekiguchi. It is possible that Takeuchi also began flying a Hei at this time, having passed his Ko on to another pilot at Cape Gloucester.

On 21 December the 68th lost its stalwart ace Shogo Takeuchi. That day he flew one of eight Hiens led by Sentai commander Maj Kiyoshi Kimura that were providing top cover for bombers targeting the Allied landing at Arawe, on the south coast of New Britain. The Japanese strike force consisted of eight Ki-48 'Lily' light bombers of the 208th Sentai, with a close escort of 12 'Oscars' from the 59th and 248th Sentais flying at 5000 ft and the eight Hiens from the 68th Sentai flying above them.

Four P-47s of the 8th FG's 340th FS attacked the Japanese formation between Cape Gloucester and Arawe, and in the dogfight that ensued

Hiroshi Sekiguchi claimed five victories over China and Nomonhan before serving with the 68th Sentai in New Guinea, where he claimed a further two kills. Sekiguchi was injured for the second time in a flying accident in February 1944 and evacuated to Japan, which probably saved his life (*Yasuho Izawa*)

Takeuchi tried to cover Kimura but received damage to his Hien. Takeuchi managed to fly the Hien back to one of the advanced airstrips at Hansa Bay, but as he descended to land his engine seized or stalled and he crashed into trees and overturned. Although extracted from the cockpit alive, Takeuchi had suffered serious injuries and died three hours later. His final score of 46 included 30 destroyed or damaged victories claimed with the 64th Sentai and 16 over New Guinea. He was also credited with ten probables. Although posthumously promoted to major, Takeuchi never received the individual citation proposed for him.

The following day both units rose from Wewak under the leadership of 78th Sentai CO Maj Akira Takatsuki to intercept approaching B-25s, but in cloudy conditions they became separated and were unable to maintain radio contact. Climbing hard, Takatsuki's formation emerged from cloud above the rear element of the 80th FS escort of 17 P-38s at 10,000 ft and used its advantageous position to bounce the Lightnings. WO Tokuyasu Ishizuka downed the P-38H in the No 4 position flown by 2Lt H B Donaldson (42-66640). Ishizuka is one of the least known of the Hien aces over New Guinea despite having survived the campaign with claims for 23 victories. As the Ki-61 pilots attempted to egress from the combat they were countered by P-38s turning back into the fight. Ace Maj Edward 'Porky' Cragg latched onto Takatsuki, who attempted a loop to turn the tables but was hit by fire from a P-38 in the following flight when almost motionless at the top of the manoeuvre. Takatsuki bailed out but Cragg's propeller and right wing sliced through his parachute and, to the P-38 pilot's horror, the 78th Sentai commander fell to his death.

Sgt Kajinami also participated in this engagement, being part of a formation of seven 2nd Chutai Hiens led by 1Lt Inoue that intercepted two waves of B-25s from the 345th BG targeting the airfields at Wewak and Boram at low level. He was again flying as wingman to MSgt Matsui, who was himself at the controls of a Mauser cannon-armed Hei. Matsui dived from 3000 ft after one of the B-25s skimming the waves, and Kajinami saw hits on the bomber's port inner wing. He then joined Matsui in attacking a second Mitchell, before becoming separated from his leader and finally attacking a third – probably B-25D-1 41-30080 *Little Stinky* of the 501st BS flown by 1Lt E E Bailey, which received fatal damage. Although there were no other Mitchell losses over the target, several of the bombers were badly damaged and had to force land upon returning to base, with three of them being written off. The USAAF reported that most of the damage had been caused by anti-aircraft fire over the target, although several aircraft appear to have received 20 mm Mauser cannon hits in the running battle.

The 68th Sentai's 3rd Chutai was also airborne in an attempt to intercept the B-25s, its leader, Lt Akinori Motoyama, and wingman Cpl Furuhashi heading a second element consisting of Sgt Iwao Tabata and Cpl Okada. Without radio direction from the ground,

Shogo Takeuchi of the 68th Sentai in formal uniform. The rank tabs on his collars are for a second lieutenant and the metal badge on his right pocket was awarded to all officer pilot graduates prior to this decoration being abolished in 1940. The zigzag insignia denotes that Takeuchi was assigned to the IJAAF (*Yasuho Izawa*)

Again photographed during an Allied bombing raid, this 68th Sentai Ki-61 has its cockpit and engine protected against the elements by a canvas cover. Note also the drop tank/bomb shackles under the wings (*US National Archive*)

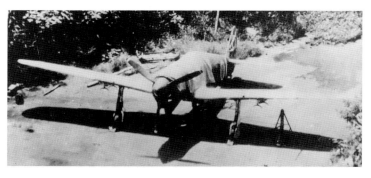

68th Sentai Ki-61-I Ko '263' was found abandoned but intact at Tuluvu airfield, Cape Gloucester, when US forces landed there on 26 December 1943. It was later repaired to flying condition for evaluation. Sometimes described as the aircraft assigned to Shogo Takeuchi, the fighter's command band is usually interpreted as white with red borders. However, close examination reveals that the lighter colour was painted over a dark-coloured band. The 2nd Chutai colour was red, so it is probable that this Hien was flown by Takeuchi with a red command band and then handed down to another pilot when the ace began flying a Hei (*US National Archive*)

A fine profile view of Hien '263' after repair at TAIC (Technical Air Intelligence Centre) 9 at NAS Anacostia, in Washington, DC, where, during January 1945, it was evaluated against the Wildcat, Corsair, Hellcat, Tigercat and Bearcat. Previously, it had been flown in Australia as XJ003, but tests were suspended when bearing metal was discovered in the engine oil. The aircraft was finally written off in a belly landing on 2 July 1945 (*via Osprey Publishing*)

Motoyama's Shotai were searching amongst the cloud formations for the American bombers when Tabata noticed smoke from the ground at Wewak. He flew up alongside Motoyama to signal him to turn back, and shortly after doing so they ran into the escorting P-38s. Furahashi dived away and Tabata moved into position on Motoyama's wing to protect his leader, but the enemy force was overwhelming and the two Hiens were soon sent down in flames, forcing Motoyama and Tabata to bail out with wounds. Both of them were subsequently rescued, although Motoyama had been so badly injured that he died of his wounds in a naval hospital on 25 December. 1Lt J L Myers in P-38H 42-66631 *My Gal Sal* failed to return after claiming one of the 'Tonys', the pilot being seen to ditch in the Sepik river estuary. The 80th FS claimed five Ki-61s destroyed and one probable.

At least one Shotai of the 68th Sentai was operational from Rabaul during December 1943 and the early months of 1944, as 'Tonys' were encountered by RNZAF and US Navy fighters during this period and also photographed on the ground at Vunakanau airfield in serviceable condition, with the tail emblem of the 68th clearly visible. On 24 December during a fighter sweep over Rabaul, Flt Lt M C P Jones of No 16 Sqn RNZAF claimed a 'Tony' as a probable. It had dived onto the tail of another Kittyhawk, allowing Jones to pull in behind the IJAAF fighter and fire a long burst down to a distance of just 25 yards. He then pulled up over the 'Tony' and felt the jolt of an explosion beneath his fighter, although no damage was later found. However, there were no corresponding fatalities from the 68th Sentai on that date either.

Sgt Kajinami subsequently had the opportunity to fly one of the Mauser cannon-equipped Hei. In mid-January 1944 he was in the air over Wewak on a combat air patrol when he received a warning that a single B-24 was approaching from the east. Spotting the enemy bomber almost immediately, he made a frontal run on the Liberator but without effect. Following up with a second run from above and behind, again without result, Kajinami then flew beneath the bomber just as its bomb-bay doors opened. Pulling sharply up, he fired a short burst from 300 yards with his 20 mm cannon. Kajinami saw some flashes where his rounds hit and debris falling away from the B-24, before the bomber suddenly disintegrated in a fierce explosion of black smoke. As Kajinami turned sharply away to avoid the blast, he saw three parachutes going down – one man with his hands raised in surrender and the other two clearly dead, one of them a headless corpse.

During his service in New Guinea Sgt Kajinami claimed eight officially recognised aerial victories and another 16 unofficial probables or damaged for a total of 24, including six P-40s, five P-38s, a P-47, a F6F, a B-24, a B-25 and a C-47. In February 1944 he returned to Japan, where he was assigned to ferrying duties, attaining the rank of warrant officer and surviving the war to become a civilian flying instructor. Flying light aircraft well into the 1980s, Kajinami later confided to his wife that he thought the reason for his survival in New Guinea was down to three factors – firstly, the one-to-one fighter pilot training he had received at Akeno and from Akiro Okada, secondly, the robust and well protected Hien, and thirdly, the fact that he couldn't drink Sake (the Japanese rice wine)! Many of his contemporaries at Wewak drank heavily in the evening to alleviate their stress, and Kajinami believed it affected their performance. Rather than imbibing, he spent his time out of the cockpit carefully reviewing his combat performance and tactics, making notes and fixing in his mind the best manoeuvres and responses to enemy aircraft to improve his combat flying.

On 15 January 1944 12 Hiens of the 68th Sentai provided cover for eight 'Oscars' from the 248th Sentai that were strafing Gusap airfield in the Ramu valley. After leaving the target area the Ki-43s would cover the 68th as it in turn let down to strafe and bomb Nadzab. WO Takashi Noguchi of the 3rd Chutai became separated from his own Shotai in bad weather en route to Gusap and arrived over Nadzab ahead of the main force. Deciding to attack alone, he made two strafing attacks before running into two C-47s descending to land at the field. Noguchi fired at the first transport aircraft and thought he had shot it down, but his attack had only damaged the C-47 and wounded a crewmember. Out of ammunition, he veered at the second C-47 with the intention of forcing it to crash into the rising jungle-clad hills surrounding the field. As the transport swerved away from his Hien, Noguchi thought he had succeeded in making it crash – this C-47 was also able to land safely, however. On his return to base, Noguchi claimed one C-47 destroyed and one probable.

Noguchi had served in the Army for almost ten years, originally in the

Keiiji Takamiya arrived in the 2nd Chutai of the 78th Sentai as an inexperienced second lieutenant, but in six months over New Guinea he claimed 17 victories. Takamiya was killed in a night-landing accident at Wewak on 1 February 1944 (*Yasuho Izawa*)

This 78th Sentai Hien appears to have flipped over in a landing accident. Could it be Keiiji Takamiya's aircraft? (*Aviation Chief Radioman Arthur Berkovitz of VPB-34 via Cris Shapan*)

Another view of the same Hien attracting some attention (*Aviation Chief Radioman Arthur Berkovitz of VPB-34 via Cris Shapan*)

Five Hiens lined up and vulnerable as Dagua is attacked by Allied aircraft in February 1944. The nearest displays a simplified tail marking attributed to the 68th Sentai, with white indicating the 1st Chutai (*via Darryl Ford*)

cavalry, before volunteering for the IJAAF. He was an instructor at Kumagaya and Tachiarai flying schools prior to being assigned to the 68th Sentai in April 1942. In New Guinea he survived a forced landing at sea and an encounter with P-38s that saw his Hien hit 54 times.

Shortly afterwards the rest of the Hiens strafed the strip, optimistically claiming ten or eleven P-40s and P-47s destroyed, together with several large aircraft. Sasumu Kajinami, who participated in this later attack, also claimed another C-47 destroyed. A total of 11 aircraft were damaged in the attack according to USAAF records.

On 16 January Noguchi's luck ran out when he was part of a large formation of IJAAF fighters that ventured over the Allied landings at Saidor, at the mouth of the Nankina River on the north coast of New Guinea. Fifteen P-40s from the 8th FG's 35th FS that had been providing protection for vessels supporting the assault climbed towards the Japanese fighters as they approached at 15,000 ft. The Warhawks engaged the formation just as an element of 'Oscars' dived on the landing area. In the confused dogfight that ensued, the 68th Sentai's Hien pilots believed they were engaging P-47s rather than P-40s. Noguchi fired at a Warhawk flown by Lt A Winton, hitting its right wing and causing him to dive away steeply in a twisting evasion. Noguchi thought he had downed the P-40, but Winton recovered from his dive and headed home, his guns inoperable. Sentai commander Maj Kiyoshi Kimura, possibly flying an 'Oscar', was then shot down and killed by the 35th FS CO and Red Flight leader, Capt G S Goolsby.

As Noguchi attempted to go to the aid of Kimura, turning tightly onto the tail of his victor, Goolsby's wingman, Lt G C Holder, called out a warning and went for the intruding 'Tony'. Noguchi spotted the P-40 coming in from behind and broke of his pursuit. He tried to dive away, but Holder followed the Ki-61 down and began firing at it until he was within 50 yards of the fighter, hitting the wing roots and fuselage. Noguchi's Hien burst into flames and he took to his parachute, falling into the sea unconscious amongst the Allied ships. He was picked up by a destroyer to become a PoW and would survive the war – Sgt Masaru Kawamoto was also lost in the fight. The returning Hien pilots thought Noguchi had destroyed two P-40s before being downed himself. His attributed final score of 14 was in reality 12, as both Winton and Goolsby survived his attacks. No P-40s were lost during the fight.

On 18 January a sweep over Wewak by 33 P-38s of the 475th FG clashed with a large force of Ki-61s and Ki-43s. The loss of three Lightnings during this engagement has sometimes been attributed to the inline-engined Japanese fighters. Sgt Shinsaku Aiko of the 78th was reported as being shot down by a P-38, which he in turn shot down, but it is more likely that he suffered a collision with a Lightning during combat. Aiko, apparently grappling with a technical problem with his propeller or engine, had dropped out of a formation of 12 'Tonys' flying at 19,000 ft right into the path of Lts W T Ritter and J Michener of the 432nd FS, who were about ten miles west southwest of Wewak.

According to Michener, Ritter then flamed the 'Tony', which pulled up sharply to the right just as the P-38H (42-66554) was passing on that side. The Ki-61's right wing was hit by Ritter's left wingtip and the two aircraft tumbled, the P-38's wing shearing off. Aiko bailed out, and on the ground he wrestled with and overpowered an American pilot who had also parachuted down, taking him prisoner. The latter was probably Ritter, although Michener never saw him bail out and he was never seen again.

The right wing of 2Lt J A Robertson's 431st FS P-38H 42-66545 had been hit by a belly tank dropped from one of the higher-level Lightning flights when 11 miles west of Boram, and although he bailed out into the jungle below he too was never seen again. Lt J R Weldon of the 431st FS also failed to return after the flight led by future ace Maj M M Smith was bounced by two 'Tonys' as it was manoeuvring to attack a larger formation of Japanese fighters below. The Ki-61s were too close for Smith to turn into them so he pushed over sharply to evade. Weldon, his wingman, was about 150 yards behind him when he took evasion action. After a steep dive and zoom-climb Smith found himself alone. He had last seen Weldon's P-38H 42-66534 at 15,000 ft south of But with a Japanese fighter within firing range of his tail.

Throughout January, February and early March the 68th and 78th Sentais continued to make sporadic low-level hit-and-run strafing attacks against the airfields at Nadzab and Gusap, as well as conducting desperate air defence sorties over their own airfields at Wewak. On 1 February the 78th Sentai's 17-victory ace Keiji Takamiya was killed at Wewak in a night landing accident, such attrition continuing to rob the Hien Sentai of experienced pilots. Combat also frequently [*text continues on page 42*]

A 78th Sentai Otsu, found abandoned in the kunai grass at Hollandia, is examined by US personnel in April 1944. The fin and tailplane bands could be yellow or light blue (*via Osprey Publishing*)

COLOUR PLATES

1
Ki-61 second prototype serial number 6102 flown by Maj Yoshitsugu Aramaki, Mito, Japan, April 1942

2
Ki-61-I Ko serial number 388 of Sgt Susumu Kajinami, 2nd Chutai, 68th Sentai, Kagimigahara, Japan, September 1943

3
Ki-61-I Ko serial number 263 of Capt Shogo Takeuchi, 2nd Chutai leader, 68th Sentai, Cape Gloucester, New Britain,

4
Ki-61-I Ko '56' of Sgt Iwao Tabata, 3rd Chutai, 68th Sentai, Wewak, New Guinea, Late 1943

5
Ki-61-I Ko '15' of the 1st Chutai, 68th Sentai, Dagua, New Guinea, February 1944

6
Ki-61-I Ko 'Ki' '19' of the 78th Sentai, Boram, New Guinea, October 1943

7
Ki-61-I of the 78th Sentai, Dagua, New Guinea, February 1944

8
Ki-61-I unit unknown, Dagua, New Guinea, February 1944

9
Ki-61-I Otsu 'Wa' of the 78th Sentai, Wasile, Halmaheras, early 1944

10
Ki-61-I Tei of Capt Takefumi Yano, 55th Sentai, Komaki, Japan, summer 1944

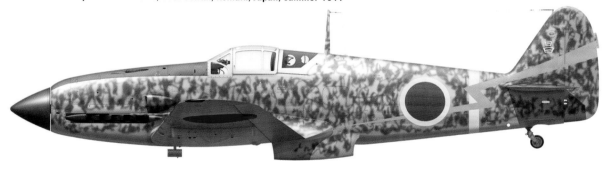

11
Ki-61-I Otsu of 1Lt Takumi Fukui, 2nd Chutai, 50th Sentai, Heho, Burma, March 1944

12
Ki-61-I of WO Takeo Tagata, Rensei Boukutai No 1, 8th Rensei Hikotai, Heito, Taiwan, October 1944

13
Ki-61-I Tei of 2Lt Takeo Adachi, 55th Sentai, Komaki, Japan, December 1944

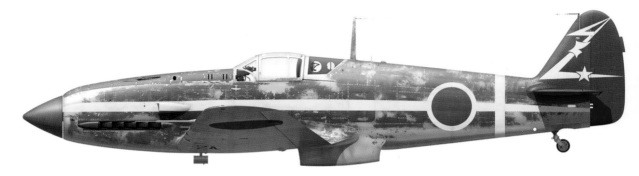

14
Ki-61-I Tei '24' of Capt Teruhiko Kobayashi, 244th Sentai Hombu, Hamamatsu, Japan, December 1944

15
Ki-61-I Hei '295' of Capt Teruhiko Kobayashi, 244th Sentai Hombu, Chofu, Japan, January 1945

16
Ki-61-I Tei '24' of Capt Teruhiko Kobayashi, 244th Sentai Hombu, Chofu, Japan, February 1945

17
Ki-61-I Tei '24' of Capt Teruhiko Kobayashi, 244th Sentai Hombu, Chofu, Japan, March 1945

18
Ki-61-I Tei '62' of Capt Teruhiko Kobayashi, 244th Sentai Hombu, Chofu, Japan, April 1945

19
Ki-61-I Tei '87', 244th Sentai, Akeno, Japan, April 1945

20
Ki-61-I Otsu '33' of Cpl Matsumi Nakano, 244th Sentai Shinten Seikutai, Chofu, Japan, December 1944

21
Ki-61-I Ko '16' of Sgt Matsumi Nakano, 244th Sentai Shinten Seikutai, Chofu, Japan, February 1945

22
Ki-61-I Hei '15' of Cpl Seichi Suzuki, Mikazuki-tai, 244th Sentai, Hamamatsu, Japan, January 1945

23
Ki-61-I Otsu '16' of Capt Fumisuke Shono, Soyokaze-tai Leader, 244th Sentai, Hamamatsu, January 1945

24
Ki-61-I '57' of 2Lt Shoichi Takayama, 5th Shinten Seikutai, 244th Sentai, Chofu, Japan, January 1945

25
Ki-61-I Hei of 1Lt Mitsuo Oyake, 18th Sentai (6th Shinten Seikutai), Kashiwa, Japan, January 1945

26
Ki-61-I Tei '50' of 2nd Chutai, 55th Sentai, Sano, Japan, August 1945

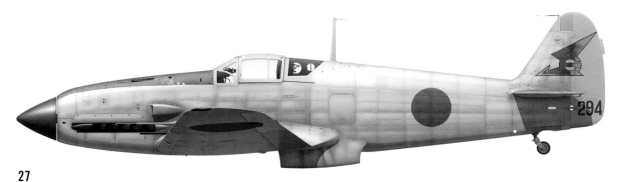

27
Ki-61-1 Hei serial number 3294 of the 56th Sentai, Itami, Japan, December 1944

28
Ki-61-1 Tei '751' of Maj Yaruyoshi Furukawa, 56th Sentai, Itami, Japan, December 1944

29
Ki-100 Otsu of Capt Teruhiko Kobayashi, 244th Sentai Hombu, Chiran, Japan, May 1945

30
Ki-100 Otsu of Maj Yohei Hinoki, 2nd Daitai, Akeno Kyodo Hikoshidan and 111th Sentai, Akeno, Japan, July 1945

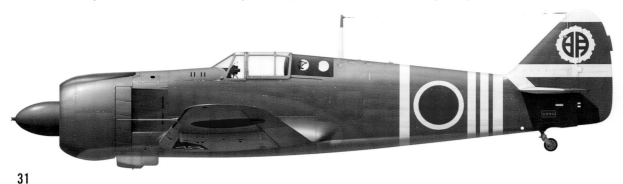

31
Ki-100 Ko of Maj Toyoki Eto, 1st Daitai, Akeno Kyodo Hikoshidan and 111th Sentai, Akeno, Japan, July 1945

32
Ki-100 Otsu of 1Lt Mamoru Tatsuda, Akeno Kyodo Hikoshidan and 111th Sentai, Akeno, Japan, July 1945

33
Ki-100 Otsu of Capt Totaro Ito, 3rd Chutai, 5th Sentai, Kiyosi, Japan, summer 1945

34
Ki-61-I Otsu '22' of Sgt Shuichi Kaiho, 39th Rensei Hikotai, Yokoshiba, Japan, July 1945

35
Ki-100 Ko serial number 16153 of the 3rd Chutai, 59th Sentai, Ashiya, Japan, October 1945

36
Ki-100 Ko of Capt Haruo Kawamura, 3rd Chutai Leader, 18th Sentai, Matsudo, Japan, August 1945

resulted in one or two IJAAF fighters being shot down and a handful of pilots returning wounded or in damaged aircraft. Despite these losses, there was little evidence that the enemy was being hurt.

Furthermore, the airfields the fighter Sentais operated from were now under almost constant air attack. Col Rinsuka Kaneko, an IJAAF staff officer at Rabaul, estimated that Japanese aircraft losses were 30 per cent from aerial combat, 50 per cent from the attacks against airfields and 20 per cent from accidents, technical failures or navigational errors. 'I can remember some occasions when entire flights failed to return', Kaneko recalled.

On 4 March, as a Shotai of 68th Sentai Hiens swept over Gusap at low level in a hit-and-run strafing attack, 1Lt Kazue Yamamoto's Hien was caught by the CO of the 41st FS/35th FG, Maj W McDonough, whose P-47 was approaching to land, wheels down. As Yamamoto passed in front of McDonough, the latter retracted his undercarriage, turned in behind the Japanese fighter and fired a short burst. The Hien pulled up steeply and then dropped straight down into the ground, thus giving McDonough his fifth, and last, victory. The remaining three 'Tonys' were engaged by Lts P Lorick and E Park as they egressed from the attack, the P-47 pilots subsequently claiming two victories. Only WO Kinji Hirahara failed to return, however.

Air defence sorties in response to USAAF attacks on the airfields at Wewak also continued, and by 7 March the 68th was down to just three serviceable Hiens and the 78th had lost its seven-victory ace Lt Mitsusada Asai in combat the previous day. On 9 March the 6th Hikoshidan reorganised in the face of these losses and in expectation of an Allied offensive. The two Hien Sentai were combined together and designated as the 1st Kogekitai (Attack Unit) under the command of the former 3rd Chutai leader of the 78th, Capt Ryoichi Tateyama.

The swansong for the two Hien Sentai in New Guinea came on 15 March when the 26-victory Nomonhan veteran 2Lt Shogo Saito failed to return from an intercept mission, the victim of ranging P-38s of the 475th FG's 433rd FS or P-47s of the 49th FG's 9th FS, or possibly a turret gunner of

Another 78th Sentai Hien in a revetment at Dagua during the devastating 3 February 1944 raid. The IJAAF admitted the loss of 57 aircraft on this date (*via Darryl Ford*)

Mitsuyoshi Tarui, who was another Nomonhan ace that flew with the 68th Sentai over New Guinea, added ten victories with the Ki-61 to his prewar score of 28. This formal portrait of him wearing his medals appears to show the insignia of a captain, but Tarui was only promoted to that rank posthumously. Close examination reveals that extra stars have been added to the image. In New Guinea Tarui held the rank of first lieutenant (*Yasuho Izawa*)

The ignominious fate of so many Hiens abandoned in New Guinea – dismembered in a dump and stripped by souvenir hunters. Both of the fighter's fuselage Hinomaru have been carefully cut out and purloined (*TSgt Jerome Schrenk via Barry Kazmer*)

This abandoned Hien was found in 1951 in an overgrown revetment at the airstrip on Jefman Island, off the western tip of New Guinea (*Luud Baier*)

a 312th BG A-20. Recorded as missing in action that day, Saito was later reported to have died in ground fighting on 2 July 1944, so it is possible that he had bailed out, perhaps injured, and found his way back to his unit.

From 16 March after a series of concentrated attacks on the Wewak airfields, the IJAAF withdrew its units (not all 68th Sentai personnel were evacuated, however) westwards to Hollandia, using the former as a staging base only. The Allied pressure continued to build, and as the IJAAF attempted to reinforce its units to regain the offensive, a major strike on Hollandia was planned. In response to that threat the 4th Kokugun commander, Lt Gen Teramoto Noriichi, ordered IJAAF units to move out of Hollandia to Noemfoor and Biak. Made aware of this through the interception of radio messages, the Allies brought forward their attack and the airfields were hit with devastating force on 30 March.

By 5 April the 68th had been reduced in strength to just four Hiens and 16 pilots, of whom only four were considered first rate. The 78th could field a paltry five Hiens and 14 pilots. There was a final reinforcement of 36 Hiens to both units at Wasile, in the Halmaheras, the following day, but reported strengths on 20 April for the two units of three and six aircraft, respectively, make it seem unlikely that the new fighters were ever delivered or moved into the combat zone.

The last 68th Sentai pilot lost in aerial combat over New Guinea was the 1st Chutai leader, Capt Toshio Takenawa, who was downed on 12 April when he led five Hiens into battle with P-38s of the 80th FS over Hollandia. He was perhaps wounded in the encounter and not evacuated, because his death was not reported until July 1944. On 23 April the 78th's 2nd Chutai leader, Capt Kenji Takahashi, was lost. The personnel who could not be evacuated were ordered to stay behind and fight as infantry, including 38-victory ace Mitsuyoshi Tarui of the 68th Sentai (who claimed at least ten kills in New Guinea and survived three forced landings in Ki-61s that had suffered mechanical failures). Tarui was reportedly killed by strafing US fighters whilst retreating on foot on 18 August 1944.

A Tony burns on the ground at Kamiri strip in the Netherlands East Indies after an attack by A-20s on 21 May 1944. Japanese attempts to reinforce New Guinea were choked off by relentless Allied attacks on IJAAF airfields (*US National Archive*)

In May 1944 the remnants of the two Ki-61 Sentais at Wasile were formed into an ad hoc fighter-bomber group under Lt Kawakami with just ten Hiens and 'Oscars', 23 pilots and 30 mechanics. In July 1944 both Sentais were formally disbanded, thus bringing to an end the year of the Hien in New Guinea.

From May 1943 to July 1944 the 68th Sentai had recorded a total of 32 pilots killed in aerial combat, including two Sentai COs and four Chutai leaders, three killed in flying accidents and one listed as a PoW. The 78th recorded the loss of 27 pilots between July 1943 and July 1944, with five Chutai leaders killed. These loss listings are incomplete, however, for the deaths of some pilots of corporal rank were not recorded at all.

CHAPTER THREE

ATTRITION

The 17th and 19th Sentais were constituted as Ki-61 units on 10 February 1944, forming the 22nd Hikodan. The 19th was transferred to Manila in March 1944 and then briefly moved to Ambon, with a detachment at Miti, in the Halmaheras, from June to August 1944 in anticipation of the Allied invasion of Morotai. The 17th went to Manila from Japan in June 1944. On 21 July orders were issued for Sho-Go (Victory) operation No 1, which set out plans for the combined defence of Leyte and its surrounding waters. By September 1944 the 17th and 19th were back together within the 22nd Hikodan, which formed part of the 2nd Hikoshidan under the 4th Army Air Force, and had moved from Manila to the airfield at La Carlota, on the west coat of Negros.

When the Allied campaign to liberate the Philippines commenced both units were under strength, with the 17th able to deploy 23 fighters, of which only 15 were combat ready. The 19th Sentai had 24 fighters, of which only five were combat ready. Their combined strength of 47 Ki-61s was less than the 56 fighters authorised for a single Sentai, and despite a desperate attempt to fly in replacement aircraft, the number available for operations at any one time was barely more than a single Chutai.

During preliminary air battles over Manila on 21 September 1944 the 17th lost ten aircraft and nine pilots whilst the 19th lost 11 aircraft and six pilots, including the Hikotai leader Capt Noritake Yano and the 2nd Chutai leader Capt Tsuneto Fukuyuma. By the end of September the 19th

A Hien of the 19th Sentai in late-war solid camouflage. This relatively new unit was brigaded with the 17th Sentai and sent to the Philippines, where both were virtually annihilated (*Yasuho Izawa*)

had only eight Hiens available. The following month the 17th lost four more pilots, including its 1st and 3rd Chutai leaders, whilst the 19th had 12 pilots killed, including the 1st Chutai leader. By 23 October the 19th had only one airworthy Hien, and the following day its CO, Maj Rokuro Seto, was killed in an air raid. The unit had now lost all of its officer pilots.

At the end of October the 19th's few surviving pilots were evacuated via Taiwan to Komaki, in Japan, where the unit was re-formed with new aviators and replacement aircraft. The 19th returned to Taiwan at the beginning of January 1945 with a compliment of 30 Hiens, sending a Chutai-strength detachment back into the maelstrom of the Philippines. The Sentai subsequently lost most of its remaining aircraft and pilots in special attack missions during the Okinawa campaign (see Chapter 4).

The 17th soldiered on in the Philippines until December, losing a total of 32 aircraft between 20 October and 25 November, before being evacuated back to Japan.

No Hien aces or notable pilots are recorded for either the 17th or 19th Sentais whilst operating in the Philippines.

In November 1944 the 18th and 55th Sentais were sent to reinforce the Philippines from Japan and placed under the temporary command of the 2nd Hikoshidan. The 18th had been formed on 27 December 1943 under Maj Rinzo Isokuza at Chofu, in Japan, from components of the 244th Sentai, with the Ki-61 as original equipment – the unit did not complete its establishment until 11 February 1944, however. The 55th was a more recent creation, forming with the Ki-61 under the leadership of Maj Shigeo Iwahashi in Taisho, Japan, at the end of April 1944.

During their deployment to the Philippines both Sentais maintained reduced strength base units in Japan, which continued to train pilots on the Ki-61 and fly home defence sorties (see Chapter 5). Both units were also virtually annihilated in the Philippines, the 55th losing seven pilots and Maj Iwahashi during its first combat on 24 November 1944. The surviving

17th Sentai tail insignia on a Hien with an unusual camouflage pattern on the fuselage. The red and white colours were used by the whole unit with the individual Chutai distinguished only by the colour of the spinners (*Yasuho Izawa*)

This intact Ki-61-I Tei of the 19th Sentai was found abandoned in the Philippines. The cowling on the Tei was lengthened by 20 cm so as to allow the aircraft to be 'up-gunned' with the Ho-5 20 mm cannon. The 19th Sentai had an inauspicious record in the Philippines campaign, with little opportunity to demonstrate the qualities of the Hien in combat (*US National Archive*)

personnel and aircraft from both units were incorporated into the 19th Sentai's detachment prior to final evacuation to Taiwan on 21 January 1945. Capt Masaji Tsunoda of the 18th Sentai, who had remained in Japan, recalled that only the Sentai commander, Maj Isozuka, deputy commander Fujinami and the 3rd Chutai leader, Capt Haruo Kuwamura, returned from the Philippines after three months of combat there. The 55th's only known ace in the Philippines was 2Lt Kesashige Ogata, who reportedly claimed five P-38 kills, but the precise details of these victories remain unknown.

Another 19th Sentai Ki-61 found in the Philippines after the Japanese surrender. This is also an early production Tei, with depot-applied green mottle over its natural metal finish (*US National Archive*)

BURMA

On 23 February 1944 the 50th Sentai, a Ki-43 unit operating from Heho, in Burma (see *Aircraft of the Aces 85* for further details), was ordered to familiarise itself with the Hien with a view to re-equipping and training

A pair of Hiens abandoned on Negros, in the Philippines, probably from the 55th Sentai. Both aircraft are camouflaged in the late-war solid olive brown scheme introduced after June 1944 (*US National Archive*)

A Hien of the 37th Kyoiku Hikotai (Training Development Air Unit). This unit, which transitioned fighter pilots from basic flying training to operational training, was formed in Taiwan, moved to Java and eventually ended the war at Matsuyama (Songshan), in Taiwan, providing a supplementary air defence capability (*Yasuho Izawa*)

with the new fighter in Saigon during the monsoon season, which was due to begin in May (and which reduced air operations on both sides). The 3rd Chutai had already acquired some experience of operating liquid-cooled inline-engined fighters by flying a handful of captured P-40s in the air defence role.

1Lt Takumi Fukui, who was acting 2nd Chutai leader, flew to Singapore to collect the unit's first Ki-61, returning to Heho on 9 March. He subsequently attempted to make the first flight from Heho in the fighter on the final day of that month, but a coolant leak and rising engine temperature prompted him to open the radiator whilst still taxiing and it was damaged when it struck the ground, forcing him to abort the sortie. The first flight was made successfully the next day.

On 4 April the Japanese airfields at Heho and Aungban were raided by P-38Hs of the 459th FG and P-51A Mustangs of the 1st Air Commando Group (ACG). The 50th Sentai had unsuccessfully sortied to intercept the raid, after which its pilots were ordered to land at Aungban because the damage inflicted on Heho had left the airfield unusable. When Aungban was raided by the ACG Mustangs the Sentai's sole Ki-61 was spotted and claimed destroyed by 1Lt John Meyer on one of his five strafing runs over the airfield. It was also subsequently claimed as damaged by 1Lt Paul G Forcey who attacked the airfield when pilots providing top cover for the raid were also called down to strafe.

On 17 April Lt Fukui was killed flying an 'Oscar' in combat with P-38s, suggesting that the Ki-61 had indeed been destroyed or badly damaged in the attack at Aungban. Three days later, the 50th's maintenance officer, 2Lt Mizuno, returned to the unit after completing a course on the Ki-61. On 27 April Sgt Yuushin Naitou was despatched to collect a second Ki-61. On 3 June two members of the groundcrew, 1Lt Sei and Sgt Yanagimichi, were also sent to the Flight Technology Institute at Singapore to attend a month-long course on Hien engine maintenance.

In the meantime the unit had discovered that the Hien was not suited to operations in Burma, as the fighter's underslung radiator was found to be too vulnerable to damage caused by stones kicked up as the aircraft taxied and took off from rough airstrips in-theatre. Another issue for the Sentai was the increased maintenance complexity of the Ki-61's inline engine, so the unit decided that it would instead replace the Ki-43 with the Ki-84 Hayate (Hurricane), codenamed 'Frank' – another air-cooled, radial-engined type.

A Ki-61 under new ownership in China at the end of the war. The original Japanese unit insignia on the tail has been crudely over-painted, making identification difficult, but it was probably allocated to one of the Shinbu-tai special attack units that were formed late in the war (*via Osprey Publishing*)

JAVA AND SUMATRA

The 37th Kyoiku Hikotai (Training Development Air Unit), also known as the 37th Sentai, was established with the Ki-61 at Pingtung, in Taiwan, on 25 February 1944. Tasked with undertaking fighter pilot training, it moved to Bandung, in Java, in May of the same year. The unit was based at Matsuyama, on the island of Shikoku, in Japan, by the end of the war.

The 18th Rensei Hikotai (Training Transformation Air Unit) was established at Bandung on 13 October 1944, and it moved to Palembang, on Sumatra, in April 1945. Here, it was combined with elements of the 7th Rensei Hikotai to provide a Ki-61 air defence capability for the nearby oil installations. The unit was disbanded on 1 August 1945 and its remaining assets transferred to No 7 Rensei Hikotai.

Would-be Ki-61 pilots progressed from the Renshu Hikotai (Training Transformation Air Unit), which provided them with basic flying training in dual control biplanes, to the Kyoiku Hikotai, where they flew the Ki-27 in both its single- and two-seat (Ki-79) variants. Here, student pilots were also introduced to the fighters they would eventually fly in combat such as the Ki-43 and Ki-61. Finally, in the Rensei Hikotai, student pilots received advanced operational training and were taught combat tactics.

The Rensei Hikotai were also frequently used to provide an auxiliary air defence capability.

Following the Japanese surrender in September 1945, there were reported to be six Ki-61 aircraft at Malang (Singosari) and four at Magoewo (Djokjakarta), which were duly seized for the nascent Indonesian air force AURI (Akngkatan Udara Republik Indonesia). There is little evidence that they were flown under their new colours, however.

CHINA

The 5th Rensei Hikotai was formed at Sunchia, in Manchuria, in May 1944 with a mixed compliment of Ki-43 and Ki-61 fighters, together with Ki-36 'Ida' and Ki-51 'Sonia' army co-operation and assault aircraft. It later transferred to Nanking and Yangsun, in China, with detachments deployed to Hangchow, Suchow and Hsihang.

On 8 December Hiens from this unit were encountered over Ta Hsiao-Chang airfield, in Nanking, by P-51Cs of the 74th FS. USAAF pilots 1Lts J W Bolyard (a future ace) and H C Cole each claimed a Ki-61 destroyed, with two more being damaged. On 25 December the 74th claimed five Hiens destroyed, three damaged and a probable over Ta Hsiao-Chang and Ming Ku Kung airfields.

In early 1945 12 Hiens from the 5th Rensei Hikotai were formed into a special attack unit under the command of 2Lt Hayato Tanaka, completing their training in China before moving to Chiran, in Kagoshima Prefecture, as the 110th Shinbu-tai in May 1945 (see Chapter 4).

No pilots achieved ace status or notable victories whilst flying the Ki-61 with the 5th Rensei Hikotai. Some of its surviving Hiens fell into Nationalist Chinese hands at the end of the war, but there is little evidence of them being flown on operations.

The Nationalist Chinese Air Force allocated its captured 'Tonys' to the 18th Fighter Squadron within the 6th Fighter-Bomber Group, but it was unlikely that they were ever flown in action against the communists (*San Diego Air & Space Museum*)

CHAPTER FOUR

THE NOOSE TIGHTENS

B y October 1944 two advanced flying training units based in
Taiwan (then known as Formosa) – the 6th Rensei Hikotai,
formerly the 106th Kyoiku Hiko Rentai (Educational Flying
Battalion) at Taichung (also known as Taichu), in the northwest, and the
8th Rensei Hikotai, formerly the 109th Kyoiku Hiko Rentai, at Heito
– had formed composite ad hoc interception units. They were both
equipped with Ki-43 and Ki-61 fighters under the command of Capt
Saburo Togo, an 11th Sentai Nomonhan veteran and 22-victory ace who
had served as a flying instructor at the IJAAF's Air Academy. The
composite units consisted of experienced instructors and the best student
pilots from both units.

The 8th Rensei Hikotai, which had been engaged in the operational
training of pilots using the Ki-27 and Ki-43, performed a subsidiary
nocturnal air defence role. In August 1943 it received five examples of the
new Hien fighter.

One of the 8th Rensei Hikotai's most experienced pilots was WO Takeo
Tagata, who had initially served as a groundcrew maintenance corporal
prior to earning his wings at Akeno in 1937 and flying the Ki-10 in combat
in China for two years. When the Pacific War broke out he was serving as
a flying instructor, but in early 1942 he was transferred to the 77th Sentai
to fly the 'Nate' in combat over Burma. Here, he witnessed the loss of more
than half the veteran pilots in the unit (see *Aircraft of the Aces 103* for

Identified as a former special attack
aircraft of the 149th Shinbu-tai awaiting
disposal at Ashiya in October 1945, this
Hien has the diagonal band of the 59th
Sentai on the fin and what appears to be
an Akeno symbol beneath the bomb and
kikusai (floating chrysanthemum) emblem
on the rudder. In addition to these specially
formed units, regular fighter squadrons
provided volunteer cadres for suicide
attack and escorted them to their targets
(*National Museum of Naval Aviation*)

further details). In May 1943 Tagata resumed his duties as a flying instructor, initially with the 8th Rensei Hikotai, although he later taught Luftwaffe-inspired 'rotte' tactics of fighting in pairs as part of the ad hoc Rensei Boukutai (Training Air Defence Unit) No 1 – a Hien-equipped sub-unit formed to provide local air defence capability in addition to performing its normal training duties.

WO Tagata's first impression of the Hien was that it was much heavier than the 'Nate' or 'Oscar' he was used to, faster in a diving attack and agile enough to hold its own in a dogfight. Indeed, it was probably better than the Hellcat in that regard. However, he was wary that the Ki-61's wings could be seriously damaged by violent manoeuvring, with loosened or sheared bolts causing the wings to collapse. On this point, Tagata's opinion differed markedly from that of Susumu Kajinami.

On 12 October 1944 carrier-based aircraft from the US Navy's Task Force 38 began a series of attacks on northern Taiwan, and fierce aerial battles raged for a number of days. During the morning of the 12th 50 aircraft attacked Heito from the direction of Niitakayama, and recently promoted Maj Togo, flying a Ki-61, led 13 Hiens and 'Oscars' aloft to intercept the raid. Bouncing an enemy formation, Togo's ad hoc defence unit was able to make only one pass before having to evade a superior number of US Navy fighers that duly downed two pilots.

WO Tagata and his wingman Sgt Matohara had been unable to take off due to hydraulic problems with their Ki-61s, and although these were resolved within 20 minutes, they were ordered to remain on the ground. Both pilots were eventually scrambled to intercept a second formation of 40+ enemy aircraft approaching Heito. WO Tagata recalled;

'We were at much higher altitude than the enemy formation and made the first attack on 36 Hellcats about 20 km from Shouka. The purpose of my first attack was to scramble the enemy formation, but my wingman (this was his first combat, although he had accumulated more than 1000 flying hours) was too aggressive and shot down a Hellcat. Though briefly surrounded by Hellcats, we successfully escaped their encirclement and regained an advantageous position. For the following 15 minutes we fought advantageously as a "rotte" against the Hellcats. Of course two against thirty-six is quite one sided, but well trained pilots flying in a "rotte" can be very effective. And varying degrees of skill amongst many pilots does not always lead to an advantage. In 20 minutes of fighting Matohara became more accustomed to combat, soon learning when to pursue the enemy and when to take evasive action.'

Tagata used the performance of the Hien to both evade and attack during this engagement;

'I dodged and started climbing so that I could attack from above. I increased my speed to 370 mph – the Hien was 25 mph faster than the Grummans, and I used this advantage to the full. I flew at more than 385 mph from time to time. I now made a sharp turn. Matohara was following me at a distance of 55 yards. Good fellow! I raised my arm in a gesture of praise. He banked his wings to thank me. I caught the lead aeroplane of the enemy formation at a distance of about 90 yards. There was a gush of gasoline from its left wing. It dived, trailing a white mist, then flew eastward. I had no time to ascertain what happened to that aeroplane.'

So far the two Hiens had received no damage, but after 30 minutes of combat evading the Hellcats attempting to encircle them, both pilots were becoming tired and losing concentration. WO Tagata's Hien came under fire, taking hits in the armour plate behind his seat;

'Then I received several hits in my wings and fire erupted, with the loss of some panels. Matohara thought my Hien had exploded, so he fled to Heito at maximum speed and very low altitude, making an emergency landing there without any injury. I made a head-on attack against the Hellcats and evaded just before collision, making an emergency landing in a nearby rice field. My landing speed was 250 mph, and I made a hard turn to stop the fighter, with the cushion against my head. I got out of the cockpit quickly and ran across the rice field to seek shelter behind a stone wall. I was shot up (on the ground) by the Hellcats, but no bullets hit me.'

During this epic fight WO Tagata believed he had been able to shoot down or fatally damage no less than 11 Hellcats, with Matohara also shooting down one and damaging four more! US Navy records do not support those claims, which were not officially recognised by the IJAAF. VF-18, however, had been badly bounced during one of its early sorties, losing three Hellcats. A fourth pilot had to bail out of his badly damaged F6F upon returning to USS *Intrepid* (CV-11). VF-18's Aircraft Action Reports (AARs) tally in some details with WO Tagata's account, the Hellcat pilots commenting on the 'beautiful way the Japanese pilots had flown their aeroplanes in pairs'. However, the Japanese fighters were identified as 'Zekes' (A6M Zero-sens, possibly mistaken for 'Oscars'), rather than 'Tonys' or 'Oscars'. 'Tonys' were identified correctly in other VF-18 AARs from 12 October, however, so the actual details of the confused combats on this day remain questionable.

Tomio Hirohata was a veteran pilot of the 59th Sentai who accumulated most of his 14 victories flying the Ki-43, although he also flew the Ki-61 during the Okinawa campaign, as shown here. He was killed on 22 April 1945 after bailing out of his Hien when he encountered engine problems shortly after takeoff (*Yasuho Izawa*)

OKINAWA AND THE SHINBU-TAI

Tokubetsu kôgeki (special attack) was a Japanese military euphemism for the tactic where aircraft would be deliberately used as manned flying bombs to destroy Allied ships, the pilots expected and expecting to die in the attempt. Towards the end of 1944 the Japanese military determined that special attacks would be the most effective way to destroy Allied surface fleets threatening invasion of the home islands. In pursuit of this doctrine they began to form Special Attack Units (Tokubetsu Kôgeki Tai was usually abbreviated to Tokkôtai), and undertook the wholesale conversion and preparation of all types of aircraft with which to conduct such operations, including the Hien. In addition, dedicated IJAAF suicide units were formed and given the designation Shinbu-tai (Shinbu or Shimbu, which meant 'stirring the martial spirit', and tai, which meant unit).

When US forces launched the invasion of Okinawa on 25 March 1945 the Japanese responded by implementing their Ten-Go (Heavenly) operation that had been planned for the defence of Taiwan and the Ryuku Islands. This combined IJAAF and IJNAF operation included a series of suicide attacks against US ships flown mainly from Chiran and other airfields in southern Kyushu. Although attacks were scheduled to be flown from Kikai-ga-Shima on the first day of Ten-Go, for suicide volunteers of the Hien-equipped 59th Sentai a series of attacks codenamed Kikusui (Floating Chrysanthemum) 1 to 10 did not commence until 6 April. They continued until 22 June, by which time 1465 sorties had been flown, 605 (41 per cent) of them by IJAAF pilots that had been directed to attack transport ships where possible. An additional 200 IJAAF special attack sorties were flown from airfields in Taiwan. The Ten-Go missions, which were accompanied by conventional dive-bombing and torpedo attacks, accounted for 26 ships sunk and 164 damaged.

A Hien of the 105th Sentai. This unit was engaged principally in special attack and escort missions from Chiran and Ishigaki during Ten-Go (Yasuho Izawa)

Participating in this deadly assault were Hien-equipped Shinbu-tai, Ki-61 escort fighters and suicide volunteers from regular Hien units. From Taiwan the remnants of the 17th and 19th Sentais undertook escort and special attack missions against US ships off Okinawa. For example, on 22 April 1945 2Lt Kuniomi Watanabe from the 3rd Chutai of the 19th Sentai sortied against US Navy ships in Kadena Bay in a bomb-carrying 'Tony' from Yilan airfield in Taiwan.

The 105th Sentai was formed at Taichung, in Taiwan, in August 1944 under the command of Maj Cho-ichiro Yoshida, with the Ki-61 as original equipment. It worked up on the Kawasaki fighter at Akeno from September to October 1944 before returning to Taichung. The 23rd Dokuritsu Hiko Chutai (Independent Air Squadron) was formed at Tachiarai, in Japan, in January 1944 under Capt Hideo Ueda from elements of the 244th Sentai, and the unit was deployed to Heito and Taichung, in Taiwan, for air defence sorties under the control of the 105th Sentai. Both units were heavily engaged in suicide operations during the battle for Okinawa, providing escort cover for Ten-Go aircraft and undertaking special attack sorties against US ships. Indeed, Hiens of the 105th were responsible for the attack on USS *LST-599*, carrying personnel from VMF-322, on 3 April 1945. One of eight special attack Hiens, escorted by five others, dived into *LST-599*'s deck, destroying much of VMF-322's equipment and wounding 21 personnel. USS *LCT-876*, which was being carried on the LST, was also seriously damaged. The 105th finished the war in Taiwan.

These 55th Sentai Hiens were photographed at Sano at war's end, all but '03' being camouflaged in the late-war solid scheme. After the main strength of the 55th had participated in the Philippines campaign the unit moved to southern Kyushu, from where it participated in the Ten-Go (Heavenly) operation over Okinawa. By August 1945 its strength was the 20 Hiens seen here (*Yasuho Izawa*)

Some sources refer to the 23rd Dokuritsu Hiko Chutai as a Hien operational training unit, but its true origin of purpose is obscure. Although displaying a similar tail marking representing a stylised '23', it is not to be confused with the 23rd Sentai that flew the Ki-44 (see *Aircraft of the Aces 100*).

On 12 April 1945 the 56th Shinbu-tai was formed with the Hien within the Hitachi Air Training Division, and it conducted sorties from Chiran against US Navy ships sailing off Okinawa on 6, 11, 25 and 28 May.

The 110th Shinbu-tai, equipped with 12 Hiens, was formed from within the 5th Rensei Hikotai under 2Lt Hayato Tanaka (see Chapter 3). On 25 May 1945, after completing training at an airfield near Beijing, the unit moved to Chiran. The following day it launched an attack on US Navy ships off Okinawa. Two aircraft from this unit crashed into the sub-chaser USS *PC-1603* moored at Taka Shima, one hitting the port bow and the other the starboard side. Neither bomb carried by the Ki-61s exploded as they passed through the thin walls of the vessel's hull. Nevertheless, three sailors were killed and 15 wounded, whilst the 300-ton ship was determined to be a complete loss after it was towed back to Kerama-retto islands, 20 miles southwest of Okinawa.

CHAPTER FIVE

A DESPERATE BATTLE

I t was in the air defence of Japan that the Ki-61 finally reached something like its true potential, flying from permanent airfields with established maintenance facilities and enjoying the benefits of easier logistics for repair and spare parts.

The first B-29 raids were launched from China, day and night, and XX Bomber Command analysed the results of the initial 25 missions, from Yawata in June 1944 to Omura in January 1945, to assess the effectiveness of the Japanese air defence. The focus on actual B-29 losses tends to underestimate the extent and intensity of the aerial combat over Japan. There had been 2200 Japanese fighter attacks, 87 per cent of them over the target and 58 per cent after bombs had gone down. Only 11 per cent of the attacks were coordinated and 41 per cent were delivered from head on, which proved to be the most destructive to the B-29s. Only 16 per cent of the attacks were delivered from the rear quarter, with rear gunners claiming 19 per cent of defensive kills. There was no hesitation in concluding that the fighter attacks had been aggressive, with 42 per cent pressed to within 250 yards, and increasingly closer until air-to-air ramming became prevalent.

Of the 18 B-29s credited to Japanese fighter attacks during this initial period, 11 were downed conventionally by gunnery passes. There were 154 air-to-air bombing attacks resulting in the loss of two B-29s. The stage was set for an increasingly desperate defensive campaign as larger and more

'As other B-29 groups came in, one after the other, the sky was painted with numberless white contrails streaming out from enemy and friendly aircraft. I have no words to describe its fierceness.' A lone Ki-61 curves in to attack a B-29 formation high in the sky over Japan (*via Osprey Publishing*)

frequent B-29 raids were launched from the Mariana Islands. The Hien would play a significant role in these missions.

For the IJAAF staff charged with the air defence of Japan the prospect of intercepting the B-29 Superfortress was daunting. Doctrinally, heights of 26,000 ft had been considered to be 'high altitude', and Japanese aircraft engines were designed to achieve their maximum efficiency at 16,000-18,000 ft. At the time the IJAAF considered that the Ki-61 had the best high-altitude performance of its single-engined fighters (the twin-engined Ki-46 was considered even better). During their training pilots attempted to attain the heights that the B-29s would operate at over Japan, but the experience was sobering. IJAAF staff officers duly concluded that it would be almost impossible to intercept the Superfortresses with the aircraft and levels of pilot ability then available. This conclusion was reinforced by attempts to intercept the first B-29 reconnaissance flights that appeared over Japan.

Only the very best pilots, rated as Class A (those with the most experience and flying hours), could be expected to fly successfully at heights of 30,000-32,000 ft. In addition to the issues of pilot ability, there were aircraft maintenance problems to contend with and frequent trouble with oxygen regulators.

EARLY WARNING

Although there is a general perception that the Japanese were deficient in early warning and ground-controlled interception, the actual situation was rather different. Coastal radar protection had been established, albeit with limitations, and there was a comprehensive network of offshore and inland observation posts connected to control centres by telephone and radio. Long-range patrolling and the specialist airborne monitoring of enemy radio traffic were also utilised. The prevalent idea that Japanese aircraft radios were poor or not much used is also misleading. Sgt Takeo Yoshida of the 244th Sentai described in his diary how radios were used for interception, with coded words and jargon similar to other air forces;

'Soyokaze, Soyokaze, Nagato, Nagato, duck whales one-zero, duck whales one-zero, east towards capital, east towards capital, umbrella eight, umbrella eight, wear high sandals, wear high sandals, end, over!'

'Soyokaze' was the squadron identity and 'Nagato' the code for Chofu airfield. With all words repeated twice, the transmission meant 'Soyakaze this is Chofu, ten B-29s flying east towards Tokyo, climb to 8000 and hold'.

SHINTEN SEIKUTAI

On 6 November 1944, inspired by reports of deliberate suicide attacks in the Philippines, the 10th Hikoshidan commander Maj Gen Kihachiro Yoshida ordered all fighter units in his division to form special attack flights for air-to-air ramming attacks against the B-29. These flights were known as 'To-Go tai' (for Tokubetsu Kôgekitai – Special Attack Unit) or Shinten Seikutai (Heaven Shaking Air Superiority Unit). Two 10th Hikoshidan units were notably exempted from this order, the 18th Sentai and the 17th Independent Air Squadron (the latter equipped with reconnaissance and armed versions of the Ki-46 'Dinah').

18th SENTAI

During the spring and summer of 1944 the newly formed 18th Sentai was working up on the Kawasaki fighter. Although the training generally went to plan, it was not without problems. Capt Masaji Tsunoda, who joined the unit in March 1944, had flown the Hien for the first time at Akeno, and he found its control column forces much heavier than those he had experienced in the 'Nates' or 'Oscars' that he had previously flown. The Ki-61 also had a much wider turning circle, and if a turn was attempted too steeply there was a danger of stalling as the wings neared the vertical.

'We practiced 15 hours a day, and gradually the number of available Hien decreased due to engine trouble', Tsunoda recalled. 'In May we sortied for mock combat practice, but during a climb to 3000 ft my engine stopped, and working the throttle lever could not overcome it. After gliding back to base, I found that the camshaft was broken'.

There were also accidents to contend with. On the last day of May, following a formal inspection of the unit by IJAAF command staff, the 1st Chutai leader, Capt Minoru Kawabata, and his wingman, 2Lt Sakagami, led a number of Ki-61s aloft into a dark sky heavy with rain. 'Soon after they disappeared into the thick clouds, a big crashing sound was heard', said Tsunoda. 'All the following aircraft were ordered to return to base, but due to the muddy airfield two aircraft turned over on landing and were severely damaged. We later found the remains of Capt Kawabata's aircraft near the Tama River and that of 2Lt Sakagami's in the middle of nearby mountains. It seemed that Sakagami had hit the tail of Kawabata's aircraft in the thick clouds. Capt Kawabata was a veteran pilot, and he led us in aerial combat training [the Sentai commander, Maj Rinzo Isozuka, was from a medium bomber unit, and had no experience of air combat fighter tactics], so his loss was a heavy blow to us.'

In anticipation of air defence sorties against the high-flying B-29, the 18th Sentai practiced fast climbs and high-altitude interceptions, but also not without mishap, as again recalled by Capt Tsunoda;

'We were told that B-29 formations would be coming in at very high altitude (30,000-32,000 ft), so we hastily practiced interceptions at such heights. At first, climbing up to 32,000 ft was not easy, but after a month of practice we could finally get up to that height. Then we practiced a mock combat, with 1Lt Iwatani's aircraft acting as a B-29. He flew at 25,000 ft and I made a frontal attack from 28,000 ft. At a distance of about 80 yards [from him] I tried to make an evasive right turn, but my Hien went straight at him! I managed to miss him by about 30 ft, and learned that at high altitude the ailerons were slow to react. When we returned to base he was really angry, yelling at me "Are you trying to kill me!?".'

By October, when the 18th Sentai moved to Kashiwa, it was officially reported to have a strength of 30 Hiens, but was still officially categorised as 'newly organised', with its combat ability below the required standard. In November, despite this lack of readiness, the main force of the unit was urgently sent to reinforce the Philippines, where it was practically wiped out (see Chapter 4). Tsunoda remained in Japan with 2Lt Oyake in the cadre unit training young pilots, and when the 2nd Chutai leader, Capt Norio Shiraishi, was killed in the Philippines on 25 November, Oyake was appointed as his replacement.

The Ki-61 was not the easiest aircraft to taxi, and this unknown 18th Sentai pilot has run into a parked aircraft. Images of 18th Sentai Hiens are rare (*Yasuho Izawa*)

Mitsuo Oyake was born in March 1914 in Tochigi Prefecture, and graduated from the Kumagaya Flying School in February 1938. He entered the IJAAF Flying School in June 1942 and after graduation in November that same year he was appointed to the rank of second lieutenant. Assigned to the 18th Sentai in February 1944 when it became operational at Chofu, Oyake would later claim a total of four B-29s shot down – one of them by ramming – and three damaged whilst flying with the unit, earning him the award of the Bukosho (Japan's Medal of Honor).

On 3 December 1944 the 18th rose to intercept the 86 B-29s of Mission 10 that had been sent to attack the Musashino engine factory. Masaji Tsunoda was flying in a two rotte quartet of Hiens with Oyake;

'On 3 December a big formation of enemy aircraft came to attack the Kanto area, and 1Lt Oyake and his wingman, myself and Cpl Memita took off to intercept it. We spotted eight B-29s at an altitude of 28,000 ft, and Oyake's rotte made a right turn to chase it from behind, while our rotte made a left turn to make a head-on attack. Oyake attacked one B-29, but the distance between them was increasing. Our rotte, at an altitude of 30,000 ft, was much better placed for the attack, and I rolled over and reversed to make a head-on diving pass [at about 60 degrees] against one B-29 with all of my guns. After evading to his tail I observed a white stream of fuel leaking, and then a few fires broke out, which eventually broke the wings from the fuselage. I reported one kill to our base. After returning to base I noticed that I had only fired my 20 mm cannon.'

The only B-29 lost over the target was 42-24656, flown by the CO of the 500th BG, Col R King. Its demise was attributed to a head-on single pass attack flown by the CO of the 244th Sentai, Capt Teruhiko Kobayashi, during his first engagement, and whose aircraft was damaged by return fire. According to eyewitness Maj J R Van Trigt, King's B-29 was attacked a few minutes after leaving the target by a 'Hamp' (A6M3 Zero-sen) in a 'one o'clock high' head-on attack that damaged the bomber's No 2 engine. Two large pieces of metal were seen to fly back and then smoke mixed with gasoline began to stream from the inner section of the left wing. It was last seen in a 30-degree dive at 24,000 ft, with wheels down and bomb-bay doors open, black smoke pouring back from the feathered engines and the wing on fire as it came under attack from up to 12 enemy fighters.

At the end of December 1944, after participating in conventional interceptions of the first B-29 raids against Tokyo, Oyake proposed that the 18th should also be allowed to form an air-to-air ramming unit. This was agreed and the 6th Shinten Seikutai was formed from within the 18th Sentai the following January.

On 7 April 1945, in perfect weather, the B-29s attacked two targets in Japan. The 313th and 314th Bomb Wings (BWs) hit the Mitsubishi aircraft engine works in Nagoya from an altitude of 20,500 ft whilst the 73rd BW attacked the Nakajima aircraft plant at Musashino, in Tokyo, from a lower altitude, escorted for the first time by long-range P-51 Mustangs from Iwo Jima.

On that day Oyake was flying at 29,000 ft over the Tama River area when he spotted the 73rd BW formation coming in at 18,000 ft. Making several attacks on a B-29 while being pursued by one of the P-51 Mustang escorts, Oyake hit the bomber several times during his attacks. It did not catch fire, however, so Oyake then made a 'taiatari' (body blow) ramming attack against the bomber's tail. After losing its tail section, the B-29 fell away and crashed in the Tokyo suburb of Kugayama, while Oyake managed to bail out of his fatally damaged and spiralling Hien, landing unhurt near a cinema in Sangenjaya. From the crash location of the B-29 rammed by Oyake, his victim was most likely to have been 42-24600 *Adam's Eve* of 500th BG. However, the loss of this B-29 has been attributed to a ramming attack by 2Lt Takashi Kawano of the 244th (see *Osprey Aviation Elite 5 – B-29 Hunters of the JAAF* for further details). It was seen to roll over near the target, with Japanese fighters in the vicinity, although the Missing Air Crew Report (MACR) does not mention a ramming attack.

There were two other B-29 losses that day attributed to ramming attacks. B-29 42-65212 *Mrs Tittymouse* of the 498th BG was rammed by 2Lt Satohide Kohatsu of the 244th Sentai, who survived the attack (see *Osprey Aviation Elite 5 – B-29 Hunters of the JAAF* for Kohatsu's personal account), but the MACR states that the bomber's left wing was shot off by flak. B-29 42-65350 of the 29th BG was reportedly rammed over Nagoya by a Ki-45. B-29 42-24674 of the 499th BG was damaged in attacks by fighters and then struck by a phosphorous bomb over Tokyo, the aeroplane exploding in midair and crashing in Choshi-shi. B-29 44-69669 of the 29th BG was reportedly brought down by flak over Nagoya, the bomber going down in a flat spin after its left wing was shot off. B-29 42-65350 *City of Muncie* of the 29th BG was also rammed by a fighter and had its left wing sheared off. The similarity of the reports suggests that the demise of a single B-29 was perhaps attributed by multiple witnesses as different events. Two 18th Sentai Hien pilots were killed intercepting the bombers, Sgt Yasuo Heima in a ramming attack and 2Lt Hideo Kojima in unknown circumstances.

The 7 April mission witnessed the most intense air combat, belied by the relatively small number of B-29s actually lost. The 313th and 314th BWs reported 233 separate Japanese fighter attacks, and 82 of their B-29s suffered damage. The 73rd BW recorded 531 attacks that damaged 69 of its bombers.

Another 18th Sentai pilot to distinguish himself in combat over Japan was the Philippines survivor Capt Haruo Kawamura, the 3rd Chutai leader, who would subsequently claim four B-29s destroyed (one by ramming) and five damaged whilst flying the Hien and, subsequently, the Ki-100.

Maj Furukawa briefs pilots of the 56th Sentai at Itami in readiness for another mission. All are wearing padded winter flying suits with fur collars (*Yasuho Izawa*)

55th AND 56th SENTAI

In May 1942, following the Doolittle Raid, the 18th Hikodan was formed from an enlargement and re-organisation of the 246th Sentai to provide enhanced air defence of the Central District. The Air Brigade contained a number of specialist units engaged in early warning and the coordination of interception operations, although its main function was to provide training for replacement pilots to join units overseas. In June 1944 the Air Brigade was enlarged to become the 11th Hikoshidan, incorporating the 55th and 56th Sentais and given the responsibility of providing the air defence of the Nagoya-Osaka area.

The 56th Sentai had been established in Taisho in March 1944, and the following month, under the command of Maj Yaruyoshi Furukawa, it began training with the Ki-43 as original equipment. At the end of April the unit moved to Itami to begin working up on the Hien, and in May the 56th moved to Komaki, an airfield north of Nagoya. The unit was subject to several re-deployments during the summer of 1944, and in August a detachment of 18 Hiens was sent to Tachiarai airfield near Fukuoka, in Kyushu, to operate within the 12th Hikoshidan, with a further detachment sent to Jeju Island, off the southwestern tip of Korea, to provide a capability for advance interception sorties against B-29 formations approaching from China. The main area of operations for the unit in Kyushu extended in an arc covering the northwestern approaches from Fukuoka to Omura, near Nagasaki.

Although the 11th Hikoshidan had established a comprehensive training programme to equip pilots to fight the B-29, this was disrupted by the re-deployments and the accelerated requirement for instructors and advanced student pilots to fly actual air defence sorties against the bombers.

The 55th Sentai was established at Taisho at the end of April 1944 and it began training with the Ki-43 before being gradually re-equipped with the Ki-61 for Homeland Defence operations. From May 1944 the unit operated from Komaki, and two months later it was incorporated into the newly formed 11th Hikoshidan. On 11 November the unit was placed under the direct command of IJAAF HQ, with a warning order for movement readiness. Eight days later it was ordered to Bacolod, in the Philippines (together with the 18th Sentai), where the unit became part of the 2nd Hikoshidan. The 55th was urgently needed to reinforce IJAAF ranks in-theatre in response to the Allied invasion (see Chapter 4).

A base detachment of the 55th remained at Komaki with nine pilots under the command of 1Lt Minoru Shirota for continued air defence operations within the 11th Hikoshidan, this small force claiming a number of B-29s destroyed. During December and January, when the bulk of the unit was overseas, two notable 55th Sentai pilots emerged from air defence sorties against the B-29. The unit commander, 1Lt Minoru Shirota, and 2Lt Takeo Adachi would each claim four bombers shot down, with the fourth and last victory for each coming on the same day.

The 55th finished the war at Komaki as part of the 'static' Permanently Stationed Air Defence Forces in the Central Defence Sector, the unit having 20 Hiens on strength – these had mainly been inherited from Sentais converting to other types.

Despite being single-engined fighter units, night interception capability was required for the 55th, 56th and 246th Sentais (flying the Ki-44 – see *Aircraft of the Aces 100* for further details), and the 11th Hikoshidan graded pilots according to this capability – A for those capable of flying proficiently at night, B for those capable only of daytime operations and C for those below both standards. This natural progression meant that night sorties were exclusively flown by the best pilots in these units. To support nocturnal operations the Division provided an improved infrastructure of early warning and radio command and control links.

WO Tadao Sumi was a veteran infantryman who had fought in campaigns in China before graduating as a pilot from the Kumagaya flying school in the autumn of 1942. After serving in the 244th Sentai, the 28-year-old NCO pilot was posted to the 56th Sentai in December 1944. By the time of his arrival the 56th had already been in action against the B-29s for three months, and it was again operating from Itami airfield, north of Osaka. The unit had gained valuable experience in the battle against the bombers, modifying its Hiens to achieve better high-altitude performance through the removal of wing cannon and armour, and claiming several of the bombers shot down as a result.

56th Sentai Hien ace WO Tadao Sumi, who had five B-29s and a P-51 to his credit as well as several damaged claims. He was awarded an individual citation and the prestigious Bukosho (*Yasuho Izawa*)

56th Sentai ace and Hikotai leader Capt Junichi Ogata (right) was credited with 12 victories, including four B-29s. He was killed in the early hours of 17 March 1945 when he probably collided with the B-29 he was attacking, shortly after the birth of his baby daughter (*Yasuho Izawa*)

Pilots of the 55th Sentai detachment, who remained at Komaki on Homeland air defence duties whilst the main strength of the unit was in the Philippines. B-29 killers 1Lt Minoru Shirota and 2Lt Takeo Adachi are seated far right and standing second left, respectively (*Yasuho Izawa*)

On 22 December Sumi's flight of four Hiens had claimed one B-29 destroyed and a second example damaged during a raid on the Mitsubishi factory in Nagoya. On the night of 13/14 March 1945 he was in action over a cloud-covered Osaka, where, in the space of three hours, 300 B-29s bombed by radar and burned out eight square miles of the city, killing 3000 people and leaving 500,000 homeless. Sumi claimed no fewer than four B-29s shot down and three damaged prior to him having had to bail out when he became disorientated in cloud and his Hien stalled. Hitting the tail of his fighter as he jumped from the aircraft, he experienced a heavy landing that injured his shoulder.

Only one B-29 (42-24754 of the 499th BG) failed to return from Osaka, its loss being attributed to flak. A further 13 suffered varying degrees of damage – in one case a bomber had to have both outer wing panels replaced. Some accounts refer to a second B-29 (42-24610 *Bedroom Eyes* of the 498th BG) being lost, but the circumstances surrounding its demise are disputed. During the Osaka mission a side blister blew out of this aircraft and a gunner was sucked out and seen to parachute down, which resulted in a Missing Air Crew Report (MACR) being filed. Confusingly, the group's mission log notes that this aircraft crashed on 24 December 1944! Despite these recorded incidents, the group historian reports that this aircraft survived the war, although the Individual Aircraft Record Card for 42-24610 appears to be missing.

Despite his claims not quite matching the official losses recorded by the USAAF, Sumi was awarded an individual unit citation and the Bukosho First Class (one of only a handful of pilots to receive this decoration). Returning to combat after his injury had healed, Sumi had claimed five B-29s and a P-51 destroyed by war's end. The Mustang was credited to him on 9 July 1945 whilst he was flying a Ki-61-II Kai, although no P-51s were reported lost on that day. Tadao Sumi was the only officially recognised ace of the 56th Sentai.

Another notable Hien pilot to serve with the 56th was Capt Junichi Ogata, a combat veteran from the 77th Sentai who had claimed eight enemy bombers over Burma. In action with the 56th against the B-29s from October 1944, he made claims for two destroyed and five damaged, although Ogata's actual tally is uncertain.

On the night of 16/17 March 1945 he engaged B-29s over Kobe, the enemy bombers being clearly silhouetted against the firestorm raging citywide. Three square miles were burned out, killing 8000 people and leaving 650,000 homeless. Ogata described the situation over his radio, claiming one bomber destroyed and saying he would continue attacking. He then apparently rammed, or collided with, B-29 42-24849 *Mission to Albuquerque* of the

Hiens of the 56th Sentai prepare for another air defence sortie over Japan in early 1945. Although the aircraft in the foreground was flown by Sentai CO Maj Haruyoshi Furukawa, it bore no distinctive command markings (*Yasuho Izawa*)

500th BG and was killed. The B-29 crashed near the summit of Mt Futatabi. Only 2Lt Robert W Nelson and Sgt A S Auganus managed to bail out, and in July both men were tried as war criminals and executed.

On the ground, 56th Sentai personnel witnessed a streak of light like a shooting star fall onto a B-29 illuminated by searchlights, the bomber duly erupting in a fireball. This suggests that Ogata's Hien might have been hit by return fire and fatally damaged during his attack. The incident was hailed by IJAAF command as a deliberate ramming, although the 56th had not been required to form an air-to-air ramming flight. 1Lt Shunro Wakui of the 56th had been killed ramming a B-29 on 3 January 1945 over Nagoya, after which the unit commander, Maj Haruyoshi Furukawa, expressed the frustration his pilots felt at seeing the cities where their families and friends lived being burned out and destroyed.

'It was unendurable for us in the air to see the burning cities and frightened people with no means to cope. This led the flyers to silently determine to risk their lives by using ramming tactics.' However, Ogata's wingmen believed his death was the result of an accidental collision. 'We don't think that Capt Ogata rammed intentionally, even if he was determined to risk his life for a near-ramming attack. As it was dark, even a skilled and experienced pilot could collide with his target aeroplane following a split second of misjudgement.' The same thing happened during daylight interceptions, and there was a prevalent tendency for the IJAAF command to attribute the death of pilots colliding with B-29s as deliberate rammings for morale and propaganda purposes.

During November and December 1944 the USAAF had also pondered whether the apparent rammings were intentional. 29th BG B-29 pilot Gordon B Robertson Jr recalled arguing with a debriefing officer that a collision he had witnessed was not a deliberate ramming. The Japanese fighter had come in head on and firing, dived under the B-29 and pulled up, colliding with or ramming the bomber in the slot behind. 'When I reported the ramming incident to the debriefers after landing, they recorded

2Lt Takeo Adachi paints his fourth B-29 victory marking on his 55th Sentai Hien for a claim made on 3 January 1945. He was killed in aerial combat on 19 January without achieving a fifth victory (*Yasuho Izawa*)

Pilots of the 56th Sentai scramble following another B-29 alert. The unit performed both daylight and night air defence sorties in the Hien, the nocturnal missions being flown exclusively by the most experienced pilots in specially equipped aircraft (*Yasuho Izawa*)

it as an intentional ramming. I disputed this theory and argued with them about it. If it had been an intentional ramming, he would have taken me out. Why dive under me to ram another aeroplane? I believe that he never saw the ship in the slot. The ramming had to have been completely unintentional and accidental.'

On 3 January 1945 the B-29s struck at Nagoya in a test incendiary mission, and both the 55th detachment and 56th Sentai were amongst the units intercepting. 1Lt Minoru Shirota deliberately rammed his fourth bomber, slamming his Hien into the No 3 engine of Maj W E 'Barney' Hurlbutt's B-29 42-24766 *The Leading Lady* of the 500th BG over Okazaki, southeast of Nagoya. The attack was filmed by a friend of his from a rooftop below. Although Shirota managed to bail out of his stricken Hien, he succumbed to serious injuries the following day. 1Lt Toshiro Wakui of the 56th, who did not survive the sortie and was posthumously promoted, has been credited with ramming 1Lt J W Lawson's B-29 42-24626 *Jokers Wild*, which failed to return. 2Lt Takeo Adachi, who had claimed his first B-29 on 18 December 1944 and two more four days later, also claimed his fourth, and last, B-29 on 3 January. He was subsequently killed over Nagoya on 19 January.

The 56th's commander, Maj Furukawa, described the experience of flying interception sorties at high altitude;

'On that day we started to climb to about 29,000-33,000 ft after we had first flown over Nagoya and then turned west, because the jet stream would push us eastward. At that altitude ice crystals twinkled and streamed over the fuselage to the tips of the wings. We felt the bitter cold. The oxygen flow meter indicated the highest mark. The engine was revolving at 2400 rpm but the joystick was heavy. We had to be most careful as the aircraft tended to drop [suddenly]. Once we lost altitude we would not be able to make attacks. We waited for the B-29s coming in. Soon engagements began with the first element of ten B-29s. As other B-29 groups came in, one after the other, the sky was painted with numberless white contrails streaming out from enemy and friendly aircraft. I have no words to describe its ferocity.'

On 18 March 1945 Capt Kenjiro Kobayashi took command of the re-formed 55th Sentai, and that night the unit claimed four B-29s shot down during a 290-bomber raid on Nagoya. However, there was only one Superfortress lost, 1Lt W C Shipp's 42-24797 *Jackpot* of the 505th BG's 484th BS being forced to ditch 115 miles from Iwo Jima with three engines out through flak damage. The crew was rescued from the sea the following day.

56th Sentai Hiens are refuelled between missions. The aircraft in the foreground is a Hei fitted with imported 20 mm Mauser wing cannon (*Yasuho Izawa*)

In early May 1945 there were a handful of B-29 raids on IJNAF airfields on Kyushu in support of extensive mining operations being carried out offshore. WO Isamu Ichige was serving at Tachiarai when, on 29 April, his Chutai was detached from the 56th to the IJNAF airfield at Saeki to assist in interception missions against B-29s attacking the Kansai area through the Ashizuri Peninsula. Saeki was home to a large number of aviators from the IJNAF, but contrary to the expectations of the Hien pilots, they were warmly welcomed at the airfield.

On 4 May, when five Ki-61 pilots attempted to intercept a single B-29 flying at 13,000 ft, Isamu Ichige's best friend WO Harada lost his life as a result of his Hien suffering engine trouble that soon saw the fighter catch fire. Three days later Ichige again participated in the interception of small B-29 formations targeting the IJNAF airfields;

'I climbed in a Hien to intercept them. I tried to make the first attack on the fuselage of the No 2 aircraft from its left side, but was exposed to the risk of being shot up by the No 3 aircraft, so I moved slightly aft and above this aircraft and fired several shots – apparently to no effect! I climbed away and then made a steep diving attack on its fuselage again. The B-29 leaked a white stream from its fuselage, and the aircraft suddenly lowered its nose and spiralled down to earth with black smoke from its belly. This was my only successful sortie with the Hien, as I then received a severe injury to my left thigh and was hospitalised until the end of the war. On that day several B-29s were shot down, but three of our pilots were lost and Sano airfield was almost totally destroyed, with many holes left in the runway.'

Ichige's Ki-61 was perhaps one of several aircraft that had attacked and shot down 1Lt R A Gray's B-29 42-69887 of the 505th BG's 484th BS, although its loss has also been attributed to Kawanishi N1K2 Shiden-kai fighters of the IJNAF's 343rd Kokutai. The B-29 crashed into a mountainside near Oita naval airfield. 1Lt A DeV Penn's B-29 42-65253 *Maryanna* was also badly shot up by Japanese fighters, with Penn and other crew members being wounded, two engines knocked out and cannon damage inflicted to the wings, tail and fuselage. The co-pilot took over flying the bomber, but he was forced to ditch after leaving the target area when a third engine had to be feathered. Finally, B-29 42-63549 was fatally rammed by a Kawasaki Ki-45 'Nick' during this mission.

At the end of May the 56th converted to the Ki-61-II Kai, although after the unit's first, and only, encounter with P-51s on 9 July 1945, when Lt Kazuo Nozaki and Sgt Maj Tomotoshi Fujii were lost, the remaining fighters were withdrawn from daylight operations. The unit ended the war at Itami with 22 Hiens and 48 pilots as part of the permanently stationed air defence force, having claimed 11 B-29s destroyed.

59th SENTAI

This Sentai, which had flown the Ki-43 in New Guinea, began converting to the Hien at Ashiya in April 1944. Two months later it was assigned to the newly formed 19th Hikodan in the Western Defence Sector together with the 4th Sentai (flying the Ki-45 'Nick' twin-engined fighter from Ozuki), by which time it had 25 Hiens on strength. The unit was not yet entirely familiar with the new aircraft, and considerable engine trouble was experienced. Vapour locks in the engines routinely occurred after takeoff and the fighters sometimes stalled following steep dives.

Although required to perform night defence operations, only a few pilots were considered capable of doing so and just four Hiens had been prepared for night flying. Due to engine and maintenance issues, the unit was only able to deploy seven or eight operational Ki-61s at most. Fortunately, the 59th had only a restricted area to defend – the industrial sites of northern Kyushu and the Yawata iron and steel works in particular. Although this should have limited the unit's opportunities to intercept enemy bomber formations, in practice the 59th was called upon to assist in the air defence of other cities and airfields within the Western Defence Sector. Ironically, when the first B-29 raid against Yawata was launched on the night of 15/16 June 1944, the 59th's pilots remained on the ground. They had been judged insufficiently confident in operating their Hien fighters at night or in coordination with the 4th Sentai's Ki-45s from Ozuki principally because Ashiya airfield, in the direct path of the raid, was required to remain blacked out.

The following month the 59th became part of the newly organised 12th Hikoshidan under Maj Gen Furuya, which also controlled the 4th and 47th Sentais (equipped with Ki-44 'Tojo' fighters – see *Aircraft of the Aces 100* for further details) and the 71st Sentai (flying the Ki-84).

In the early hours of 8 July the night-flying Hien pilots of the 59th were scrambled to provide a patrol screen in the path of 18 B-29s radar-bombing Sasebo, Omura, Tobata and Yawata. The Hien pilots struggled through ten-tenths cloud at just 1300 ft to reach their 10,000 ft patrol height, but failed to engage any of the enemy bombers.

In May 1945 the unit began to re-equip with the Ki-100 (see Chapter 6), and it finished the war at Ashiya with only 15 fighters on strength.

The leading Hien-flying ace of the 59th was WO Tomio Hirohata, who had served in the unit for five years. Claiming victories over Timor and New Guinea in the Ki-43 (see *Aircraft of the Aces 85* for further details). Hirohata had amassed a total of 14 victories by the time he was killed over Makurazaki on 22 April 1945, having been forced to bail out of his Hien fighter as a result of technical difficulties. Although WO Kazuo Shimizu of the 59th had a tally of 18 victories and flew the Ki-61 over Japan, the majority of his claims were also made over New Guinea whilst flying the Ki-43, where he gained fame for Ta-dan attacks. Another ace Hien pilot of the 59th was the Bukosho winner 1Lt Naoyuki Ogata, who claimed five victories, including three B-29s shot down.

71st SENTAI

Although the 71st Sentai is better known for being a Ki-84-equipped unit, in July 1945 it was re-formed with the Ki-61 as part of the permanently stationed air defence force. Indeed, it ended the war at Bofu with seven Hiens on strength. The unit's re-equipment was part of the Sei-Go plan devised by the IJAAF in May-June 1945, this strategy calling for the preparation and preservation of air power for the final defence of Japan against an expected imminent invasion. However, the continuing destruction of industrial capability by air raids forced Army Air HQ to issue an order for the Sei-Go deployment on 1 July 1945 to provide for continued air defence against air raids in the form of a permanently stationed air defence force, whilst enabling a designated mobile air defence force to react to any invasion attempt. The role of the mobile force was mainly to provide escort and counter-air (fighter versus fighter) capability for special attack sorties.

As a direct result of this order all fighter units in Japan were assigned according to aircraft type to either static defence districts (Ki-44, Ki-45 and Ki-61 units) or to mobile defence air groups (Ki-84 and Ki-100 units). Furthermore, they were to provide mutual support in emergencies.

One of the principal aims of this plan was to ease maintenance and supply issues for frontline units by basing the same aircraft types together. As a result of these changes the Ki-84-equipped 71st Sentai, formed in May 1944 at Kameyama, in Honshu, as part of the 12th Hikoshidan, with responsibility for the Western Defence Sector (and subsequently sent to the Philippines), was ordered to re-form and re-equip with the Ki-61.

ARMY AIR TEST CENTRE

During the early spring of 1945 the Army Air Test Centre at Fussa was busy evaluating the latest model Ki-61-II Kai, as well as participating in air defence missions. By this time 30-victory ace Yasuhiko Kuroe was one of its leading test pilots;

'One day [in the early spring of 1945] a formation of B-29s attacked the Kanto area, and I took off in a Hayate [Ki-84]. But before I could catch the formation, a flight of four Hiens led by Maj [Iori] Sakai, with 2Lt Takezawa as his wingman, and Capt Ito and 1Lt [Ryozaburo] Umekawa – all of them very experienced Hien pilots at the Centre – began to attack a lone B-29 from below its nose. The first shots fired by Maj Sakai hit a fuel tank, and a white stream of fuel leaked from the aircraft. The second shots by 2Lt Takezawa also hit the same area, and this time a few fires broke out. The third and fourth shots by Capt Ito and 1Lt Umekawa punched more bullets into the same area, and all of them flew up above the B-29 in a beautiful turn. Then suddenly a big explosion disintegrated the huge body of the B-29, and it fell to the ground in a fireball near Shinjuku.

'Later I heard that this crash caused more damage on the ground than several incendiary bombs, but the attack was very beautiful and had downed a B-29 in a brief sequence of shots in a short time. The only witnesses to this event were the four pilots and I, and as none of them ever boasted about this deed afterwards it was never publicly reported.'

Kuroe would subsequently claim three B-29s himself whilst serving with the Army Air Test Centre – one whilst flying the twin-engined Kawasaki Ki-102 twin-engined heavy fighter (built as a replacement for the Ki-45) and two in the Ki-84.

Maj Iori Sakai was a Nomonhan veteran who had claimed eight victories flying the Ki-27 (see *Aircraft of the Aces 103* for further details) and later became the chief test pilot for the Ki-100 (see Chapter 6), whilst Ryozaburo Umekawa was the test pilot who had first fired the Hien's guns in anger (see Chapter 1). The most successful Army Air Test Centre pilot against the B-29 was WO Isamu Sasaki, who added to his impressive record of kills over Burma in the 50th Sentai (see *Aircraft of the Aces 85* and *103* for further details) with claims for six B-29s destroyed and three damaged – three of his successes were achieved in a single night over Tokyo on 25/26 May 1945.

TERUHIKO KOBAYASHI AND THE 244th SENTAI ACES

Teruhiko Kobayashi rose to fame as the leader of the equally famous Hien-equipped 244th Sentai, and they both played key roles in the air defence of Japan. Kobayashi has begun his IJAAF career as a bomber pilot, flying an obsolete Kawasaki Ki-32 'Mary' light bomber (another liquid-cooled engine type from the Kawasaki stable) during the attack on Hong Kong in December 1941. By the time he took command of the 244th in November 1944 as the youngest Sentai leader in the IJAAF, Kobayashi had been flying for more than six years, including a stint as a flying instructor at Akeno following his promotion to captain.

Kobayashi survived the war, and after nine years working as a civilian, in 1954 he joined the Japanese Air Self-Defense Force (JASDF). He re-trained in Japan on the T-6 Texan and T-33 Shooting Star, before completing jet fighter training on the F-86 Sabre in the USA in 1955-56. On 4 June 1957 Kobayashi was flying a T-33 on a training sortie from Hamamatsu when a technical problem occurred shortly after takeoff. He ordered his companion to eject before he attempted to land, but the aircraft crashed shortly thereafter and Kobayashi was killed.

Leading the 244th Sentai, Kobayashi was to claim three B-29s and two F6F Hellcats shot down and five aircraft damaged. Despite these successes, he was not the unit's leading ace as is sometimes imagined. The leading B-29 killers of the 244th were the 3rd Chutai leader Capt Nagao Shirai,

who claimed 11 B-29s and two F6Fs destroyed, with a further six damaged, and 2Lt Chuichi Ichikawa with nine B-29s claimed shot down and six damaged, plus a claim for an F6F destroyed.

Kobayashi referred to Ichikawa in his diary as 'a god', and confided that he wanted to bow to him even though he was a subordinate officer. Ichikawa had been flying since 1937, and as a junior NCO pilot in the 9th Sentai he had just missed the fighting against the Soviets over Nomonhan in 1939. His exceptional flying skills were soon recognised, and after promotion to sergeant major he served as a test pilot at the Army Air Test Centre prior to securing a place at the Army Air Academy in December 1942. He graduated from here as an officer the following year. Ichikawa then flew briefly with the 78th Sentai over New Guinea before being wounded in action and returning to Japan – one of the lucky few to escape this theatre. In December 1943, after recovering from his wounds, Ichikawa was posted to the 244th Sentai.

Another Army Air Academy graduate, Nagao (or Takeo) Shirai served in the 244th Sentai from November 1942 and was appointed to command the 3rd Chutai in October 1944. Although he survived the war, this modest man never talked about his wartime accomplishments or participated in veteran activities, and as a result his remarkable combat record has been overlooked.

The 244th Sentai was one of the oldest home defence squadrons, being formed in July 1941 with the Ki-27 as original equipment and converting to the Ki-61 in July 1943. Initially, the unit was under the direct operational control of Eastern Army Command, charged with air defence of the critical Kanto Sector (within the Eastern District), including the Imperial Palace, the Tokyo-Yokohama area, Tachikawa and other vital strategic locations within the region.

Following the Doolittle Raid of April 1942, the 244th became one of two fighter Sentais assigned to the newly formed 17th Hikodan for administrative purposes, although it remained under the operational control of Eastern Army Command. In March 1944 the 17th Hikodan was reconstituted as the 10th Hikoshidan, removed from the 1st Air Army and placed under the direct command of the Commander-in-Chief of the

Early Hien '38' of the 244th Sentai in factory-fresh condition. This particular aircraft has been attributed to Cpl Nobuji Negishi prior to his transfer to the 18th Sentai in late 1943 and ultimately to the 53rd Sentai, where he became the unit's top ace and a Bukosho winner flying the Ki-45 'Nick' twin-engined fighter. He was credited with six B-29s destroyed and seven damaged (*Author's collection*)

Capt Nagao Shirai, leader of the 244th Sentai's Mikazuki-tai, accumulated a remarkable score of eleven B-29s and two Hellcats destroyed and six aircraft damaged but avoided publicity and never spoke about his exploits after the war. He died in 1974 (*via Osprey Publishing*)

The 244th Sentai's Soyokaze-tai in flight over Tokyo Bay on 23 February 1945. Capt Fumisuke Shono leads in '88', a Mauser cannon armed Hei adorned with a lightning bolt (*Author's collection*)

General Defence Command, whilst operational control continued with Eastern Army Command. By July of that year the 10th Hikoshidan had six fighter Sentais under its command, two of which, the 18th and 244th, were equipped with the Ki-61 and both operating from Chofu, an airfield about nine miles to the southwest of central Tokyo. By October 1944 the 244th had 40 Ki-61s on strength, and its pilots were rated as 'adequate', second only to the 47th Sentai (equipped with the Ki-44 – see *Aircraft of the Aces 100* for further details) in quality.

The unit had spent much of 1944 preparing to defend Tokyo from the B-29 raids that would inevitably come later in the year. One of the pilots involved in this period of intense training was Capt Goro Takeda, who had joined the 244th in April 1944, 'by which time the Sentai was already equipped with Hiens. Under the command of Maj Fujita we practiced night formation flying [probably the only home defence unit to do so]. The 244th Sentai often did night interceptions, but the number of pilots capable of such fighting in the dark was limited to veterans, usually four to six pilots in each Chutai.

'Initially, the 1st Chutai leader was Capt [Toyohisa] Komatsu, the 2nd Chutai leader Capt [Yoshiro] Takada and the 3rd Chutai leader Capt [Hideo] Muraoka, but these officers [including the CO, Maj Takashi Fujita] moved to other units, and the famous commander Kobayashi arrived. Chutai leadership also changed, with the 1st Chutai leader being Capt [Fumisuke] Shono, myself in charge of the 2nd Chutai and the 3rd Chutai led by Capt [Takeo] Shirai. The maintenance crews were also reorganised from [supporting] each Chutai to [providing a single] crew team for the whole Sentai. Each Chutai had about 16 aircraft and the Headquarters flight had four aircraft, so the total number would be around 52 aircraft. When it came to flying interception missions, however, each pilot tried to take off in any available aircraft, so usually only around ten fighters from each Chutai would typically be scrambled.'

The 244th operated a HQ Chutai, while the three remaining Chutai were named rather than numbered as the Soyokaze-tai (zephyr or gentle breeze unit), Toppu-tai (squall or sudden gust unit) and Mikazuki-tai (crescent moon unit). The Soyokaze-tai was the fourth Chutai of the 244th, having been established in October 1944 as a training squadron, with three experienced pilots acting as instructors. Trainee pilots in the 244th had a white band or 'flag' painted on the antenna masts of their Hiens to warn other pilots and groundcrew of their inexperience.

Red-tailed Hiens of the 244th Sentai. Aircraft of the Shinten Seikutai air-to-air ramming flight had red tails, and CO Kobayashi had the tails of HQ Shotai aircraft painted red to show solidarity (*Yasuho Izawa*)

The Shinten Seikutai or air-to-air ramming unit in the 244th was under the direct tactical command of Kobayashi, although it was formally subordinate to the 10th Hikoshidan commander and separate from the rest of the Sentai. Within the 244th, the air-to-air ramming unit was first called the Hagakure-tai (from Hagakure-Hidden in the Leaves, the collected writings of Yamamoto Tsunetomo, which became a spiritual guide for Samurai), although it was later referred to simply as the Shinten-tai. It was disbanded on 10 March 1945. Remarkably, Sgts Masao Itagaki and Matsumo Nakano of the Shinten Seikutai each made two successful ramming attacks against B-29s and survived, earning semi-hero status within the 244th (see *Osprey Aviation Elite 5 – B-29 Hunters of the JAAF* for details of their exploits).

Capt Fumisuke Shono (his surname is sometimes written as Ikuno in English language references) had been serving as a flying instructor at Akeno when he was posted to the 244th Sentai as its 1st Chutai leader at the end of November 1944, and like Kobayashi (who had been teaching at the Akeno airfield at Takamatsu) he took his own Hien with him when he joined the unit. He recalled;

'[The] B-29 attackers usually came in an altitude of 30,000 ft in daytime, but a Hien [if well maintained] could reach the same or higher altitudes. The Mauser 20 mm cannon was quite effective, with electrical charging and jam clearing. So the Hien was a very good interceptor against the B-29, the fighter shooting down more of them at night than during the day. At night, the B-29 stream usually came in at an altitude of 9000-10,000 ft, and the ground fires from the bombing made them easily visible to us from above,

Sgt Masao Itagaki, a member of the Shinten Seikutai air-to-air ramming flight, prepares to sortie in '14'. Itagaki not only survived two ramming attacks against B-29s, he also survived the war (*Kikuchi Collection via Horoshi Umemoto*)

whereas our Hiens could not be spotted so easily by the B-29 crews. So, during night interceptions, much less defensive fire from the B-29s was observed, and we could make effective attacks from the rear below [at almost the same speed]. It was, therefore, much easier to shoot down B-29s at night.'

On 19 December 1944 the 244th was sent to operate from Hamamatsu airfield as reinforcements for the air defence of the Central District following B-29 raids on the 13th and 18th. The Sentai was also required to camouflage its aircraft, groundcrew hastily applying dark green mottle to 30 aircraft in just 24 hours. Three days later CO Kobayashi claimed a B-29 as damaged during an abortive raid against the Mitsubishi aircraft factory in bad weather. This was possibly 42-24684 flown by Capt J H Darden of the 499th BG's 877th BS, whose No 3 engine was damaged in a head-on attack by a single Ki-61 after leaving the target. Although the engine was feathered, the B-29 fell out of formation and failed to return.

On 3 January 1945 a Toppu-tai Shotai led by Capt Goro Takeda and including 2Lt Kyoshi Ogawa, WO Shirobeh Tanaka and Cpl Saburo Umehara jointly claimed to have shot down a B-29 during the Mission 17 raid on Nagoya that was also intercepted by the 55th and 56th Sentais (as noted earlier in this chapter). Ogawa was referred to in the Sentai as 'little Ogawa' as he shared his surname with another pilot who was a much larger man. Ogawa was to become the first 244th Sentai pilot to be killed in combat flying the Ki-100 (see Chapter 6).

On 9 January Kobayashi and 2Lt Ichikawa each claimed another B-29 damaged during a raid against Musashino, although the CO's Hien was damaged by return fire and he had to force land. Earlier that same day Kobayashi's wingman, Cpl Kiyoshi Ando, had claimed a B-29 destroyed before he too made a forced landing as a result of damage from return fire. 2Lt Mitsuyuki Tange of the Shinten Seikutai was credited with destroying a B-29 by ramming, although he was killed in the attack. Finally, 2Lt Shoichi Takayama, also of the Shinten Seikutai, survived a ramming or collision with another B-29 and Cpl Seiichi Suzuki claimed a Superfortress destroyed.

On 27 January 1945 the 73rd BW was scheduled to target factories in either Musashino or Nagoya, depending on weather reports from pathfinder B-29s, with secondary targets of the Tokyo docks and nearby urban areas. The 244th was

Hien '71' of the 244th Sentai is serviced between missions at the Tachikawa air arsenal. Although an Otsu manufactured in early 1944, this aircraft has been painted in the late-war solid scheme, with the cartouche under the tailplane reading 'mei sai nuri ryu' ('camouflage paint') (*Author's collection*)

then still based at Hamamatsu, between the two targets, and it was scrambled to intercept the raid. Sentai commander Kobayashi, flying Hien '295' that had previously been the mount of the 1st Chutai leader Capt Komatsu, and his wingman Sgt Kiyoshi Ando, flying Hien '45', approached Col Robert Morgan's B-29 formation from their '11 o'clock' position at an altitude some 5500 ft higher than the bombers.

As the first B-29 box passed under his left wing, Kobayashi rolled over and dived from the near vertical to an angle of 45 degrees in order to target the leading bomber from the 'six o'clock high' position. Both Hiens struck B-29s as they flashed through the formation with their guns firing, Kobayashi managing to bail out but Ando was killed. Kobayashi's victim was possibly 42-65246 *Irish Lassie* flown by Capt L Avery, which was clipped in the left wing just behind the No 1 engine. Although the bomber had lost eight feet of aileron and one of its fuel tanks had been ruptured, Avery managed to retain control of the B-29 and was continuing his bomb run on the target when the aeroplane was rammed a second time in the tail. The bomber had probably been hit by the Ki-61 of 2Lt Katsumi Hattori, who was credited with his fourth B-29 but did not survive the impact. Nevertheless, the crew still managed to coax the bomber back to Saipan, where a successful crash-landing was performed.

Ando's victim was possibly 42-63541 *Ghastly Goose*, which also survived the ramming but was forced to ditch on the return flight. WO Tanaka claimed damage against another B-29, but he was so seriously wounded in this engagement that he did not fly again. 2Lt Shoichi Takayama again rammed or collided with a B-29, but this time he was killed.

Capt Takeda recalled the reality of flying against the B-29 for the first time, and also observed that ramming was not always a deliberate act;

244th Sentai commander Teruhiko Kobayashi in the cockpit of his K-61 '24', which has been decorated with his B-29 claims, including a ramming. The photograph was taken during a much-publicised visit to the unit by the famous singer Hamako Watanabe (*Yasuho Izawa*)

Groundcrew wave farewell to Hiens of the 244th Sentai HQ Shotai second element as they taxi out for takeoff. '52', probably flown by Lt Itakura, has its wing armament removed, whilst Lt Matsumoto's Hei has a spiral spinner design and red-painted tail (*Kikuchi Collection via Horoshi Umemoto*)

Lt Itakura pauses on the runway with a fine backdrop of Mt Fuji – propeller trouble? Camouflage has been removed from the tail of '52' perhaps in preparation for painting it red (*Kikuchi Collection via Horoshi Umemoto*)

'Most of the pilots did not imagine that the B-29 could cruise at [such a] very high altitude [30,000 ft] and high speed. Initially, we tried to attack from the rear [as usual], but we soon realised that the risk of being shot up was too great. We quickly changed the tactics to frontal attack. B-29 formations often approached with the benefit of a westerly wind, before turned east from Mt Fuji to attack the Tokyo area. We waited for their formations over Hachioji or Tanashi, although climbing up to 30,000 ft to intercept them took about 30 minutes.

'We shared our airfield at Chofu with an IJNAF air group, and the 244th Sentai achieved more victories than it. Several pilots successfully returned from "body crash" (taiatari) attacks against the B-29, but these were never deliberate attacks. It was impossible to align a diving Ki-61 up with a fast-moving B-29 [by doing so, the pilot greatly increased the chances of being shot up by one of the bomber's turret gunners]. In most cases they made a "life or death" attack, and by chance hit the tail or fuselage of a B-29 with a wing.'

The 244th claimed its first fighter kills when, on 16 and 17 February 1945, the fast carriers of the US Navy's Task Force 58 launched their aircraft for strikes against airfields around Tokyo. A second attack against airfields on Kyushu on 18 and 19 March resulted in further claims, as well

as losses. The 244th was credited with ten Hellcats and a Helldiver shot down, with two of the naval fighters being claimed by Kobayashi on 16 February. However, Cpl Seiichi Suzuki, who had claimed two B-29s shot down and a third shared, as well as one shared damaged, was killed in aerial combat on 16 February.

On 19 February Cpl Tomonobu Matsueda, who usually flew as wingman to Lt Tsutomu Obara, was credited with single-handedly bringing down 882nd BS/500th BG B-29 42-63494, flown by 2Lt G C

244th Sentai pilots train in the use of the gunsight. Cpl Tomonobu Matsueda, who is operating the sight, was credited with single-handedly downing a B-29 on 19 February 1945. He was subsequently made Kobayashi's wingman, but on 7 April Matsueda was shot down and killed by a P-51 (*Kikuchi Collection via Horoshi Umemoto*)

Rouse Jr. Part of a force attacking Matsushino, the bomber crashed into a primary school in the Tokyo suburb of Shinjuku – only two crewmen escaped by parachute, surviving the war as PoWs. Matsueda had attacked the B-29 repeatedly until it broke up in the air, by which time his Hien had been hit by return fire and he was forced to crash land on an army parade ground at Shibuya. From there he ran to the site of the B-29 crash and identified himself as the pilot who had shot it down.

Matsueda was subsequently killed on 7 April 1945, perhaps too intent on another B-29 victory for he was reportedly shot down by a P-51. He was possibly the first victim of future six-kill ace Capt Harry Crim, CO of the 531st FS/21st FG. He described an encounter with a solitary Ki-61, whose pilot he believed had not seen him, in his combat report as follows;

'A lone "Tony" came alongside the bomber stream some 200 yards out and was leisurely choosing his target. I was 2000 ft above him and rolled down to intercept but had too much power and overshot. I reduced power, pulled around and he was still shopping among the bombers. I took a shot at him – it didn't faze him. Then another burst from 1000 ft and I knocked off his right wing. He never took any evasive action – he was entranced with the B-29s and never knew we were there.'

On 12 April Kobayashi damaged his third B-29, but this time he was badly hit by return fire and bailed out with a leg wound.

On the night of 15/16 April the 244th scrambled its night-flying pilots against 219 B-29s whose incendiaries burned out more than three square miles of Kawasaki, six square miles of Tokyo and one-and-a-half square miles of Yokohama. Chuichi Ichikawa was up, and after shooting down two B-29s and damaging a third, he rammed a fourth bomber. He managed to bail out of his fighter, although he was injured in the process. Ichikawa was awarded the Bukosho First Class for his feat. Although some references state that Ichikawa was flying a Ki-100 (see Chapter 6), the first examples of the fighter did not reach the Sentai until 23 April. At least ten B-29s were lost during this mission to Japanese fighters or anti-aircraft fire, including 42-24821 of the 398th BS/504th BG, flown by 2Lt D M Knell. It was last seen illuminated by a searchlight beam and apparently coming under rocket attack from a fighter.

Chuichi Ichikawa, seen here as an aviation cadet, claimed nine B-29s shot down. He had risen through the ranks, flying since 1937 and being wounded serving with the 78th Sentai over New Guinea. In July 1945 Ichikawa was awarded an individual citation and the Bukosho, with promotion to captain. Having survived the war to become a civilian pilot, he was killed in a flying accident in 1954 (*Yasuho Izawa*)

A fine shot of Capt Shono's well-photographed '88'. Note the camouflaged ailerons and remnants of camouflage on the white Homeland Defence 'bandages' on the wings. 244th Sentai aircraft went through stages of being camouflaged, stripped of paint and re-camouflaged (*Kikuchi Collection via Horoshi Umemoto*)

Within the 244th the practice of removing armament and armour to improve high-altitude performance was not limited to the Shinten Seikutai. Some pilots had the wing guns stripped out, others the cowling guns and some even flew with only one cowling gun installed. The principal reason for de-arming the Ki-61 was the inconsistent altitude performance of individual aircraft, pilots being forced to modify them to achieve optimum performance. The Mauser MG 151/20 20 mm wing cannon of the Ki-61-I Hei were so highly prized that they were sometimes salvaged and retro-fitted to older model 'Tonys' (see Appendix 1).

39th KYOIKU HIKOTAI

The 39th Kyoiku Hikotai was established as a training unit on 31 July 1944 at Yokoshiba for advanced fighter pilot instruction. Equipped with the Ki-79 advanced trainer, as well as the Ki-27 and Ki-61, the unit became known as the 39th Sentai or Hien Hikotai (Swallow Air Group) after it sortied its Hiens in the air defence role towards the end of the war.

On 20 July 1945 the very young Sgt Shuichi Kaiho was on a training sortie as wingman to Sgt Iwao Tabata when they encountered P-51s attacking Tokorozawa airfield. Kaiho dived impetuously on the Mustang leading the USAAF formation and fired several bursts from his 12.7 mm wing guns, shooting the fighter down over the airfield. He later met the captured pilot, a 'Maj Jones', who had six or seven kill markings on his aircraft. The American was shocked to discover that he had been bounced and shot down by a pilot of Kaiho's apparent youth and inexperience. The true identity of 'Maj Jones' and his ultimate fate is unknown.

As previously noted in Chapter 2, Tabata had survived being shot down over New Guinea in December 1943 whilst serving with the 68th Sentai, Both he and Kaiho had also escaped with their lives after an epic dogfight with Hellcats of VF-9 and VF-45 over Yokoshiba in April 1945 whilst at the controls of open cockpit Ki-79 trainers. After Kaiho had single-handedly attacked four Hellcats, the tables were quickly turned and he was chased back towards the airfield. His Ki-79 soon resembled a flying wreck, having been badly shot up, leaving Kaiho with little choice but to force land in a 'controlled crash' short of the airfield. Thrown out of the cockpit, and losing four teeth when he hit the ground, Kaiho narrowly escaped being strafed. On a more positive note, he met his future wife in the house of the woman who came to his aid. Following these close shaves, Kaiho and Tabata regularly flew Hiens together as a rotte in air defence sorties, claiming two fighters destroyed and two B-29s damaged between them – victory symbols for their shared kills were painted onto both of their aircraft.

IJAAF CHANGES

In March 1945 Maj Gen Yoshida had been replaced in command of the 10th Hikoshidan by Lt Gen Kanetoshi Kondo. The 6th Air Army had been temporarily placed under the command of the Combined Fleet for the Ten-Go Ryukyu Islands operation, its units conducting aerial combat over Okinawa (see Chapter 4). The 30th Air Fighter Group was also formed at this time as part of a new aerial combat plan, its primary duty being to engage any enemy carrier task forces that attacked the Kanto Sector. The 30th was to provide fighter escorts and air combat capability for special attack operations against such task forces.

The 244th Sentai was transferred to the 30th Air Fighter Group, together with the 47th Sentai (newly equipped with the Ki-84), five special attack Shinpu units (18th, 19th, 25th, 45th and 47th), two reconnaissance units (17th DHC and the Shimoshizu Air Unit) and dedicated navigation aircraft in the form of three bombers from the Utsonomiya Air Training Division and two Navigation Air Squads.

As part of his strategy Lt Gen Kondo planned to husband his fighter resources. In anticipation of an increasing number of land- and carrier-based enemy aircraft appearing over Japan, he planned to refocus the employment of his fighters from air defence against bombers to fighter versus fighter combat in future operations. 'Abandon the over emphasis on training for combat against bombers and stress combat against fighters', Kondo ordered. He believed that fighter pilots trained to combat enemy fighters should have no problem tackling enemy bombers as required.

'Avoid a decisive battle with enemy fighters until the fighter versus fighter training is completed. Concentrate on protecting aircraft on the ground. Increase the capabilities and numbers of anti-aircraft guns. Make use of decoy aeroplanes to lure enemy aircraft into positions where they can be destroyed by ground fire. Ignore enemy reconnaissance aeroplanes, but make concentrated attacks on enemy formations composed mainly of bombers performing large scale bombing missions.'

This directive brought to an end the policy of air defence interception sorties against every incursion threatening a strategic target, IJAAF fighters

Another air-to-air photograph of Capt Shono's '88' as he pulls in closer to the camera aeroplane. Note the venturi on the side of the forward fuselage reportedly for a gyro gunsight. Behind Shono's Hien is the camouflaged '71' (*Kikuchi Collection via Horoshi Umemoto*)

instead engaging enemy aircraft selectively under favourable conditions. In future air raid warning data would be passed to Sentai commanders on an advisory basis, and they would have independent discretion as to when and how to engage.

'Improve supply and maintenance of aeroplanes and equipment', ordered Kondo, and this was partly achieved by grouping similar types of aircraft together in single parent formations.

On 15 April 1945 the Air General Army was established under Gen Masakazu Kawabe to take unified command of all air defence forces. In May and June 1945 the Sei-Go (Control) operation was promulgated to preserve IJAAF air power by reducing air defence sorties to a minimum so as to create a significant fighter force that was ready to oppose an expected invasion attempt on the mainland. In practice Sei-Go was not fully implemented until 1 July because the increasing damage being inflicted on Japan's industrial capacity by the B-29 offensive demanded an air defence response. All these plans came too late to radically improve the deteriorating capabilities of the IJAAF, and they were themselves subject to changes forced by unforeseen developments in enemy strategy such as the appearance of increasing numbers of escort and free-ranging fighters over Japan.

Capt Fumisuke Shono of the 244th experienced firsthand the impact escort fighters had on the IJAAF;

'The situation dramatically changed when fighters escorted the bombers. We practiced more for bomber attack than dogfighting with fighters, so we were not so [well] trained to deal with them. The Hien had cannon in the wings, which increased the radius of turn, so some pilots removed these weapons for combat with fighters. The bombers reduced their attacking altitude to 16,000 ft, but we had to first sweep out the escort fighters before attacking the B-29s. The shoot down rate decreased dramatically and our losses increased. I once fought an F4U Corsair, which probably had the same kind of performance as the Hien. It was armed with six machine guns, however, and the stream of fire from those weapons was awful.'

CHAPTER SIX

SEVEN-WEEK FIGHTER

The Ki-61-I Tei Hien continued to roll off the assembly lines at Kagamigahara in decreasing numbers until January 1945. Production of the Ki-61-II Kai was underway by August 1944, but within a month the supply of Ha-140 engines had failed to keep pace with the construction of airframes, which then began piling up. By the end of the year there were more than 200 II Kai airframes without engines. Three months earlier, realising that there was a problem, IJAAF Air HQ directed Kawasaki to fit them with Mitsubishi's 1500hp Ha-33/62 (Ha-112-II) 'Kinsei' (Venus) radial engines, which were available in large numbers. Originally, it was planned to use the engines and cowlings from Ki-102 production, but in practice the conversion utilised a newly designed cowling, fairing and propeller that were strongly influenced by the engine mounting and fairing from an imported Focke-Wulf Fw 190A-5.

The conversion was surprisingly successful and a prototype was flown in February 1945 under the designation Ki-100, although it was known by its pilots as 'Goshikisen' (Type 5 fighter) – it never received an Allied codename. Wholesale conversion of the II Kai airframes began that same month, and by the time output switched to production of 'new' Ki-100 aircraft in June 1945, 275 engines and airframes had been married up and delivered.

The 18th Sentai in the 10th Hikoshidan became one of the first units to convert to the Ki-100 in March 1945, but within four months it had only 12-15 fighters on strength – the equivalent of only a single Chutai.

The Ki-61-II Kai was a development of the Hien, with an Ha-140 engine intended to improve its altitude performance. A shortage of engines resulted in only 99 being delivered, with the bulk of the airframes being re-built as the radial-engined Ki-100. The Ki-61-II Kai was flown on air defence sorties by the 56th Sentai and Army Air Test Centre at Fussa (*San Diego Air & Space Museum*)

This close-up of a Ki-61-II Kai cowling shows latch details and the inertia starter handle. This surviving aircraft, serial number 5017, was damaged when it was put on public display at Hibiya Park, Tokyo in September 1953. Curiously, the majority of the II Kai aircraft appear to have been delivered in natural metal, although they were manufactured after olive brown factory painting was introduced (*via Osprey Publishing*)

Two other fighter units in the permanently stationed air defence forces also converted to the new fighter, the 5th Sentai in the 11th Hikoshidan and the 59th Sentai in the 12th Hikoshidan both commencing their conversions in May. The 5th had been flying the Ki-45 'Nick' in the nightfighter role, and for a brief period it continued to operate both types.

In the mobile air defence forces, the 244th Sentai in the 30th Air Fighter Group began conversion to the Ki-100 from 23 April 1945 when the first examples of the new fighter were issued to the unit. Four days later the 244th suffered its first fatality with the Ki-100 when 2Lt Tasukichi Ide crashed during a test flight. On 30 April 2Lt Kiyoshi Ogawa was the first Sentai pilot to be killed flying the Ki-100 in combat against B-29s.

The 111th Sentai was to be formed with a mixed compliment of Ki-100s and Ki-84s drawn from the Akeno Kyodo Hikoshidan (Training Air Division), which had been established at Akeno with the dual roles of training pilots to fly in combat and providing a reserve air defence capability for the Central Defence Sector. This Division had originated as a To-Ni-Go Butai (Secondary Provisional Unit) of flying instructors to augment air defence forces in the 11th Hikoshidan (see *Aircraft of the Aces 100* for further details), but it was subsequently made into a permanent unit.

The 17th Sentai in Taiwan was the only overseas unit to officially commence conversion to the Ki-100 in June 1945, although one or two examples of the new fighter were also sent to overseas commands for evaluation. Indeed, the 20th Sentai also in Taiwan received a solitary Ki-100.

Most pilots found the new hybrid fighter superior to the Hien in all respects, and Capt Hideaki Inayama, who had formerly flown the Ki-44 with the 87th Sentai (see *Aircraft of the Aces 100* for further details), opined that 'the manoeuvrability of the Ki-100 was the best of the Army's frontline fighters, with the exception of the Ki-43. Even less experienced pilots could fly it easily and fight with it'. Capt Fumisuke Shono of the 244th Sentai also welcomed the new fighter;

'In May I switched to the Type 5 fighter. This was a very good – probably the best – Army fighter. Not only was it fitted with a more reliable air-cooled engine, but it also had 20 mm cannon in the fuselage [the Hien had them in the wings], so the radius of turn was much less.'

Capt Shono's remarks about the armament are puzzling (see Appendix I). He soon had the opportunity to test the Ki-100 against the best of the American fighters then appearing over Japan;

'In early May I fought alone against eight Mustangs over Atsugi after intercepting a B-29 and P-51 formation. As I was at a higher altitude, I decided to attack them. Before I could get within firing range they released their drop tanks and took evasive action. I fired a burst at their tail end Charlie, but that was the end of my ammunition. From then on I was engaged in a one-sided fight against the eight P-51s, but I never feared being shot down due to the high performance of the Ki-100. I took continuous evasive action until the P-51s gave up chasing me, probably due to a shortage of fuel. After returning to my base I counted 24 bullet holes in my Ki-100 – compared to two or three holes usually found after fighting the B-29.'

Capt Goro Takeda was another 244th pilot who exulted in the performance of the Ki-100;

'After switching to the Ki-100 – a much better and reliable fighter – I was twice in aerial battles over Yokkaichi [the 244th's last airfield on Honshu, near Lake Biwa to the west of Nagoya]. In one of those combats we were in the air on a training mission when we spotted 12 enemy aircraft flying below us. We made an advantageous attack and shot down most of them. In my second aerial combat with the aircraft, which took place one month before the end of the war, I was chased by a Hellcat. However, when I performed a steep climb the Hellcat stalled away.'

As part of the 30th Air Fighter Group, the 244th was tasked with escorting special attackers sent to engage an expected invasion fleet, and it flew escort missions to Okinawa during April and May 1945. After his unit had re-equipped with the Ki-100 in May, Capt Shono remembered the difficulties pilots faced when undertaking long-range escort missions in the new fighter;

This view of a surviving Ki-100 shows clearly how the Mitsubishi Ha-33/62 (Ha-112-II) 'Kinsei' (Venus) radial engine was faired cleanly into the basic Ki-61 airframe (*Ronnie Olsthoorn*)

'After moving to Kyushu to protect Special Attack Units, we found that the cruise range of the Ki-100 meant that we could not go beyond Okino-erabu Island. This meant that the Special Attack Units had to fly the remaining distance [32 miles] to Okinawa without protection, and that led to them suffering heavy losses. We fitted an extra fuel tank to the belly of the fighter to increase its cruise range, but by then Okinawa had fallen into US hands.'

On 3 June the 244th took its Ki-100s into action against a force of US carrier-based fighters that were attacking the southern Kyushu airfields. Twenty Corsairs from VBF-85, embarked in USS *Shangri-la* (CV-38), attacked the airfields at Chiran (where the 244th was based at that time), Kagoshima and Tojimbara, whilst 36 Hellcats from VF-9, VF-20 and VF-46, flying from USS *Yorktown* (CV-10) and USS *Independence* (CVL-22), headed for airfields near Kanoya. MSgt Jiro Asano and Sgt Tamakake Fumihiko were patrolling at 15,000 ft when they spotted a formation of Corsairs at 16,500 ft heading south. They immediately attacked, and ground personnel at Chiran watched spellbound as Asano demonstrated the sparkling qualities of the Ki-100 in a fight with a single Corsair right above the airfield. By war's end Asano had claimed ten enemy aircraft shot down and a further seven as damaged or probables.

Sentai commander Kobayashi, who was also airborne during this engagement, was forced to crash land due to engine failure. Capt Goro Takeda and his wingman Sgt Yamashita of the Toppu-tai took off to join the fight after re-fuelling and re-arming, but they were caught by two Corsairs just moments after departing Chiran. Takeda was able to evade the attack with a tight turn, but Yamashita could not follow him and was shot down, crashing into a farm at Kawabe.

The 244th pilots claimed seven Corsairs shot down for the loss of three aircraft, with Sgt Kazuo Honda killed in action. VBF-85, however, listed only two losses in aerial combat on this date. Lt J H Shroff, whose Corsair was shot down into a forest at Nagakura, near Kagoshima, has been attributed as the probable victim of IJNAF Shiden-kai 'George' fighters from Squadron 301

Capt Totaro Ito, who was the 5th Sentai's 3rd Chutai leader, scored most of his 13 victories flying the Ki-45. However, towards the end of the war, he flew the Ki-100 and, reportedly, the Ki-61 in air defence sorties. Ito's final score included claims for nine B-29s, and he was another Bukosho recipient (*via Osprey Publishing*)

of the famed 343rd Kokutai, which also participated in these combats. Having engaged 'Tonys' and claimed three shot down and one damaged over Kagoshima Bay at 0820 hrs, the pilots from VBF-85 had been attacked 30 minutes later by four Japanese fighters that they identified as 'Tojos' (Ki-44s). Shroff had failed to return from this second engagement after becoming separated in a dive and then being heard calling for help over the radio.

Lt(jg) E Dixon of VBF-85 was also shot down, having possibly fallen victim to 2Lt Ikuta of the 244th Sentai, who forced a Corsair to crash land on the beach near Bansei airfield – he fired warning shots to prevent the pilot escaping into the surf. Ikuta reportedly met his victim shortly thereafter and the American pilot presented him with his watch. Both Shroff and Dixon survived the war as PoWs.

2Lt Jisaburo Aikawa of the 55th Sentai from Bansei (near Chiran) was possibly the victim of Lt S Lovdal of VBF-85, who subsequently crashed to his death near Chiran when the tail of his Corsair broke away just a few minutes after shooting down a 'Tony'.

VF-46 lost two Hellcats and their pilots (Lt(jg) W R Apgar and Ens R T Dyer Jr) during this mission, but those losses were attributed to bad weather encountered by the unit's fighter CAP 30 miles from CVL-22 and 85 miles southeast of Okinawa.

On 5 June Ki-100s from Akeno intercepted 530 B-29s attacking Kobe, the pilots involved claiming six bombers shot down and five probables from the nine admitted lost by the USAAF as a result of enemy action. One of three B-29s downed as they egressed the target area and attributed to the Akeno Ki-100s was 1Lt W B Palmer's 42-63451 *Black Jack* of the 444th BG's 678th BS, which had been hit in the No 3 engine by flak over the target. The engine was feathered, and as the aircraft began to lose height and fall behind it was attacked by the Ki-100s. Fifteen miles from Kobe, and with the engine blazing, the right wing broke away. The B-29 then rolled over and fell away in a nose-down spin until it crashed in the Kowaura mountains. Ten crewmen managed to bail out, but one soon succumbed to serious wounds once on the ground and the surviving nine were duly executed by Japanese personnel from the Tokai Air Defence HQ.

Capt R L Arnold's B-29 44-69665 of the 468th BG's 793rd BS was also shot down by the Akeno fighters, the bomber crashing into a forest at Otani. Nine crewmen were captured after they had bailed out, and they too were executed at the Tokai Air Defence HQ.

1Lt R A Rochat's B-29 42-24742 of the 498th BG's 874th BS came under a coordinated attack from six fighters, which shot out the No 1 engine. This caused the bomber to fall behind, allowing two more fighters to ram or collide with the B-29's tail and No 4 engine. As 42-24742 fell away out of control, the pilot and co-pilot struggled to keep the aircraft straight and level. Eventually it entered a spin, and only four crewmen (the navigator, bombardier, radar operator and engineer) were able to bail out and parachute into the sea, from where they were rescued by a US Navy submarine. The navigator of 42-24742, 2Lt John P Duffy, gave the following graphic description of what it was like in the B-29 after the initial attacks;

'We were 20 miles from land's end when our first really serious trouble occurred. The No 1 engine was hit by gunfire and it soon began to lose oil before eventually windmilling out of control. The CFC [Central Fire

Control] gunner [SSgt D G Blackwell] called out that he had been hit and his sighting mechanism shattered. The tail gunner [Sgt E L Macon Jr] then called out that his arm had been blown completely off. Fighters collided with the No 4 engine and the empennage. The tail gunner was last heard from when he asked the aeroplane commander if he could come forward as he was feeling weak and faint. The pilots were struggling fiercely to keep the aeroplane under control.

A Ki-100 Otsu of the Akeno Kyodo Hikoshidan (Training Air Division), which later formed the 111th Sentai. This aircraft was flown by 1Lt Mamoru Tatsuda (*via Osprey Publishing*)

'Suddenly I felt the ship lurch violently and slew to the right. The ship soon began to act very queerly, just flip-flopping around the sky. From my position I could see the co-pilot [2Lt A Budawei] struggling with the controls. I saw the engineer [2Lt J Z Kesches] open the nose wheel well door and the bombardier [2Lt C J Duveen Jr] come forward, prepared to jump. The co-pilot reached over and let the nose wheel down. The order to bail out was given at this time. The bombardier went out immediately. I glanced at the engineer's altimeter and it read 10,000 ft. I felt myself being thrown backwards and realised we were in a spin. The last I saw of the pilots was just before leaving the ship. They were struggling with their one-man life rafts. The radio operator [SSgt W D Lower], engineer and myself had difficulty getting out of the aircraft due to the centrifugal force.'

Capt Yohei Hinoki's Shotai from Akeno downed 1Lt D J Schiltz's B-29 44-69766 *City of Burbank – Old Soldiers' Home* of the 330th BG's 459th BS after he had initially made a solitary attack that caused the bomber to drop out of formation. The Ki-100s followed the B-29 down, and it crashed into the eastern bank of the Kizu River in Najima as Schiltz attempted to force land on the riverbed. Six crewmen managed to bail out before the crash, only to be captured and subsequently executed by the Japanese military police. The 26-year-old Capt Hinoki was an 11-victory ace from the 64th Sentai who had fought against the American Volunteer Group at the outbreak of war and lost a leg in combat with Mustangs over Burma (see *Aircraft of the Aces 13* and *85* for further details).

No fewer than 647 fighter attacks were made on the B-29 force on 7 June, resulting in the inevitable duplication of victory claims.

During July the 20th Air Fighter Group was formally established comprising the 111th Sentai from Akeno and the 112th Sentai from the Hitachi Kyodo Hikoshidan. A third Sentai was planned, but it had not yet been formed by war's end. The 20th Air Fighter Group was assigned to the mobile air defence forces, with its HQ at Komaki, in the Central Defence Sector. The 111th had been built around a cadre of experienced flying instructors (some of whom had achieved ace status in previous units) at Akeno who had already taken the Ki-100 into combat on 5 June and 16 July. The new Sentai consisted of five Chutais, divided into two Daitais (Battalions), the 1st Daitai consisting of two Chutais equipped with the Ki-100 and a third equipped with the Ki-84. The 2nd Daitai, commanded by the newly promoted Maj Yohei Hinoki, consisted of the Ki-100-equipped 4th and 5th Chutais.

The 5th Sentai was a former Ki-45 Toryu unit specialising in nightfighter operations that began conversion to the Ki-100 in May 1945, but continued to operate the twin-engined fighter until the end of the war. '39', a Ki-100 Otsu with a bubble canopy, was flown by Hikotai leader Capt Yasuhide Baba. It is seen here at Kiyoso airfield, near Nagoya, during the summer of 1945. The Ki-100s delivered to the 5th Sentai were reportedly painted dark green, and not the usual late war olive brown (*San Diego Air & Space Museum*)

Maj Yohei Hinoki, a former 64th Sentai ace who had lost a leg over Burma, later served as an instructor at Akeno and eventually commanded the 2nd Daitai (Battalion) of the 111th Sentai. His final tally of 11 victories included a single B-29 (*via Osprey Publishing*)

At 1330 hrs on 16 July the Ki-100s from Akeno and the 244th Sentai's Soyokaze-tai at Yokkaichi were scrambled in response to a fighter sweep by 96 P-51 Mustangs of the 21st and 506th FGs that had been tasked with strafing Japanese airfields in the vicinity of Nagoya. The Soyokaze-tai leader Capt Shono and his wingman intercepted the Mustangs of the 21st FG as they dropped down in preparation to strafe Suzuka airfield. Within minutes Shono's luck had run out, however;

'After the Kyushu operation the 244th Sentai had moved to Yokkaichi, where its pilots achieved many kills. Regrettably, I was hospitalised by wounds received during the 16 July mission, which was the first time I had flown the Ki-100 after a long absence [due to the Higher Command order to preserve fighters until the final battle]. One after another, the Ki-100s that I had led aloft returned to base with [technical] trouble until only myself and MSgt [Iwao] Doi remained in the air. We spotted a formation of P-51s and attacked them from higher altitude. We both destroyed two Mustangs before Doi himself was shot down, leaving me to fight on alone against many P-51s. Finally, my aircraft was shot up, and although I escaped by parachute I had by then been wounded by a single bullet.'

Capt Shono had been hit in the left shoulder and left knee, and as his parachute drifted down into a field a large crowd gathered, thinking he was an American. Capt Shono yelled loudly to them that he was Japanese. When the the Toppu-tai at Yokkaichi was informed of the loss of two of its fighters, the unit urgently scrambled more aircraft. These arrived on the scene too late to engage the enemy formation, however. Shono's leg wound was so serious – the round had a severed a nerve – he would require repeated surgery after the war.

Elsewhere on 16 July, the Ki-100s that had been scrambled from Akeno formed up at 21,000 ft, with Maj Toyoki Eto's 1st Daitai leading and Hinoki's 2nd Daitai following at a higher altitude to starboard. After flying in a southeasterly direction towards the coast, the Japanese formation turned left and flew along the southern side of Ise Bay towards the northwest. The 4th Chutai leader Capt Katsuji Sugiyama soon spotted Mustangs from the 457th and 458th FSs crossing from left to right at a lower altitude as they dropped down to join the dogfight that was already in progress between the 21st FG and the two Ki-100s of Shono and Doi over Suzuka.

Hinoki thought that the Mustangs 10,000 ft below him looked tiny, 'just like long floating strings'. Sugiyama turned in behind the P-51s and immediately dived on them. Hinoki followed, although he was experiencing problems with the propeller control unit of his fighter as he opened the throttle, causing his aircraft to skid. Nevertheless, he dived on the last Mustang in the formation, getting close enough 'until I could see – so to speak – the enemy pilot's white teeth. Even if my aeroplane skidded, I couldn't miss. I fired from 20 metres and then saw the enemy aeroplane spinning down as if in its death throes. I glanced back and there were ten enemy aeroplanes behind me'.

The P-51 shot down by Hinoki was probably the aircraft flown by Capt John W Benbow of the 457th FS, who failed to return and was reported missing in action. Capt Benbow's element had been following the lead aircraft of Capt W B Lawrence, which was in turn focused on the pursuit of another Japanese fighter. Benbow had shouted 'That's enough Bill, you've got him!' at Lawrence, urging him to leave the pursuit as the Japanese aircraft fell away on fire and broke up in the air. He was not heard from again after this radio transmission. Benbow's demise was not witnessed by the other Mustang pilots, his aircraft crashing in woodland at Katsurahata and his remains being buried at the site.

5th Sentai Ki-100s being prepared for flight at Kiyoso. Note the worn cowling on the aircraft in the background. The Ki-100 was never allocated an Allied codename, usually being identified in combat as a Ki-84 'Frank' or A6M Zero-sen (*Yasuho Izawa*)

After downing Benbow, Hinoki found himself in an increasingly desperate situation as he had to turn ever tighter to avoid the attention of the remaining Mustangs. Eventually, he dropped the nose of the Ki-100 in a near vertical dive, and when he finally pulled out he found himself alone in the air.

The Akeno pilots made claims for six Mustangs shot down and five probables, whilst the 244th claimed two. In reality, only Benbow's P-51 failed to return from the mission, although four other Mustangs were damaged. 2Lt B Robinson of the 46th FS suffered hits to his engine but was able to return, whilst 1Lt I Skansen's aircraft was almost downed by a burst of cannon fire that damaged his port wing, fuselage, fin and rudder. He too managed to get home. Future ace Capt Abner Aust of the 457th claimed three 'Franks' destroyed and two more damaged prior to being bounced and shot up – his fighter sustained hits to the wings and fuselage, destroying his radio and RDF equipment.

Overall, the Mustang pilots claimed 25 aircraft destroyed, 18 damaged and two probables. The Akeno formation lost five aircraft and three pilots, Capt Motomichi Suzuki and 1Lts Jiro Oka and Eijo Takano. The USAAF pilots acknowledged that their Japanese counterparts were 'aggressive and able', but once their initial attack broke up 'like a covey of quail', they did not coordinate with each other either offensively or defensively.

A Ki-100 Otsu in the typical factory finish of olive brown over natural metal with a plain Hinomaru (*Author's collection*)

On 25 July the 244th engaged ten Hellcats from VF-31, embarked in USS *Belleau Wood* (CVL-24), on an airfield sweep. After strafing Yokkaichi, the Hellcats had climbed to 5000 ft when they were bounced by 15 fighters the naval aviators identified as 'Franks' and 'Tonys' that dropped on them from cloud cover at 12,000 ft. Some of the Ki-100s dived away after the initial attack, but others began a series of dive-and-zoom attacks from the clouds above.

During this engagement, after reportedly shooting down one of

Ki-100 Ko of the 59th Sentai at the end of the war. Contrary to popular belief, the squadron insignia included the span-wise Chutai colours on the fighters' tailplanes, as worn by previous aircraft types flown by this unit (*Yasuho Izawa*)

the Hellcats, Lt Tsutomu Obara collided with or rammed the F6F of Ens E R White. The American fighter crashed into a rice field at Oshitate-mura, killing the pilot, while Obara bailed out of his stricken Ki-100. Having been seriously injured in the collision, he died on the ground an hour later. Obara (a promising officer who had graduated top of the 56th class at the Army Air Academy) was posthumously promoted to captain.

Ens H L Law force-landed his damaged Hellcat in another rice field at Haneda and was captured, although he survived the war as a PoW. Lt(jg) C W Robison managed to nurse his damaged Hellcat back to the carrier despite having been wounded by fragments after his canopy was hit. In addition to Robison's fighter, four other F6Fs were damaged in the clash but managed to return to CVL-24. One of them required a wing change and another had to have a propeller replaced. The jubilant Ki-100 pilots claimed 12 Hellcats shot down, while VF-31 was credited with eight Japanese fighters destroyed, three probables and three damaged. Only two Ki-100s were lost, however, with WO Ikuta having successfully bailed out.

On the night of the 1 August Capt Haruo Kawamura, the 18th Sentai's 3rd Chutai leader, brought down B-29 44-86344 of the 462nd BG's 768th BS. Flown by Capt W J Gay, it was the only one of 862 bombers attacking Japan that night to be lost. The B-29 had already suffered flak hits in the wing centre section and nose, causing a fire in the bomb-bay, when Kawamura attacked it. He made two conventional gunnery runs, and on the third pass either rammed or collided with the bomber's tail, causing the B-29 to crash near Obitsu Bridge in Sakatoichiba, Chiba-ken. Kawamura was able to parachute from his fatally damaged Ki-100 to claim his fourth B-29 victory. Although one crewman was killed during his attack, the remainder bailed out and were captured by IJNAF personnel from Kisarazu airfield. 1Lt C R Harlan put up a fight once on the ground and was killed, but the others survived the war as PoWs.

Against the scale of the assault that night, Capt Kawamura's victory in the Ki-100 was but a defiant pinprick. The bombers had dropped 1025 tons of high explosive, 5115 tons of incendiaries and 242 tons of mines, destroying or damaging more than six square miles of four cities and devastating an average of 78 per cent of their built up areas. Barely a week later the unrelenting aerial onslaught against Japan would culminate in two of the most terrible bombing raids of all as atomic weapons were dropped on Hiroshima and Nagasaki, and the Kawasaki Hien and Goshikisen would fly in combat no more.

The Ki-100-II was a turbo-supercharged development to improve altitude performance. It would have been the lightest turbo-supercharged fighter of the war, but by the time of surrender only three prototypes had been completed (*Yasuho Izawa*)

APPENDICES

APPENDIX I

Ki-61 PRODUCTION TYPES

A subject that frequently causes confusion and has sometimes been misrepresented is the variant type designations and armament arrangements of the Ki-61 Hien series. By the end of 1942 a total of 34 Ki-61s had been produced, all of them incorporating retractable tailwheels and armament consisting of two cowling-mounted Ho-103 12.7 mm machine cannon synchronised to fire through the propeller arc and two wing-mounted Type 89 7.7 mm machine guns. The Japanese Army designated any automatic weapon above 11 mm in calibre as a kikan hou or machine cannon, and whilst in the West the Ho-103 would have been classified as a heavy machine gun, it was capable of firing a variety of ammunition including high-explosive incendiary rounds that burst like a cannon shell on impact.

Various improvements in fuel, oil capacity, armour and fuel tank protection were introduced throughout the preliminary production run of what would be retrospectively designated Ki-61-I Ko machines (for an explanation of the Ko, Otsu, etc., armament suffix designations see Appendix I in *Aircraft of the Aces 100*). The basic armament was not improved until October 1943 when from serial number 501 the Ki-61-I Otsu model began to roll off the production line at Kagamigahara. This variant also had Ho-103 12.7 mm weapons installed in the wings, increasing the firepower to four machine cannon. At some point during the production run of this variant the retractable tailwheel was replaced with a fixed one. In later use some of the earlier models had the tailwheel fixed in the lowered position and the doors removed from the airframe.

During September 1943 production of the Ki-61-I Hei model commenced from serial number 3001, this model having wing-mounted German Mauser MG 151/20 20 mm cannon as special equipment instead of the Ho-103 machine cannon – a much prized improvement. The 800 German cannon had been shipped to Singapore on board the Italian submarine Aquila VI, arriving there on 31 August 1943. Production of the two Ki-61 variants then proceeded in parallel until July 1944, with a total of 592 Otsu and 400 Hei models being manufactured.

From January 1944 production of the Ki-61-I Tei model commenced from serial number 4001, which had two Ho-5 20 mm machine cannon installed as cowling weapons, requiring the engine to be moved forward by 200 mm and thereby lengthening the nose of the aircraft. A total of 1358 Tei models were produced up to the end of January 1945, and they carried the heaviest homegrown armament installed in the Ki-61-I series. Many Tei airframes had the wing armament (and cockpit armour) removed for improved altitude performance during the air defence of Japan.

An attempt to improve the performance of the Hien resulted in the short-lived Ki-61-II, which ultimately proved to be a failure. Its development was centred on the Ha-140, a second-generation DB 601 derivative powerplant intended to improve altitude performance – work on the engine had begun in September 1940. Inlet flow was improved, the supercharger strengthened, compression increased, exhaust thrust augmented and water-methanol injection introduced. However, in bench tests the new engine proved troublesome, with excessive vibration, main bearing failures and oil leakages resulting in overheating.

Again, engine development paralleled airframe development (of a longer fuselage and larger wing area), with the result being that by August 1943, when the first of eight Ki-61-II airframes was ready, there was still no engine to put in it. Indeed, a further three months would pass before initial flight testing revealed that the marriage was not a happy one in any case. Drastic modifications had to be incorporated in the Ki-61-II Kai (for kaizou, meaning modified or re-structured), including a reversion to the original wing plan. The II Kai was not ready for production until August 1944. However, for various reasons, engine production was simply unable to keep pace with airframe production, and of the 374 airframes that had been completed by May 1945 at least 208 became 'Kubinashi' (headless) without engines and had to be stockpiled.

Within this production run of the last 'Tony' variant the many complaints from pilots about the poor rearward visibility from the Ki-61 cockpit were also finally answered with the provision of a cut down fuselage and the fitting of a 'teardrop' or 'bubble' canopy. It is possible that the II Kai designation actually referred to that modification rather than the reversion to the original Ki-61-I wing design, but this is uncertain. One authoritative source reports that only 99 Ki-61-II Kai were eventually delivered with Ha-140 engines, probably not in sequential serial numbers, and that an unknown quantity of these had the 'teardrop' canopy. Some sources also assert that a number of Ki-61-II Kai aircraft were produced with provision for Ho-5 wing cannon, but the continuance of the Tei armament in the subsequent Ki-100 series suggests that is unlikely.

Subject to the engine operating properly, the Ki-61-II Kai proved to be an excellent fighter, with an impressive altitude performance. However, ongoing reliability issues and inadequate numbers prevented the variant from reaching its potential during the air defence of Japan, and it was effectively supplanted by the Ki-100. The capability of the latter machine, even as an expedient design, far outstripped expectations.

The Ki-100 was produced in two variants – the so-called Ko with a canopy arrangement identical to the Ki-61-II, using stockpiled airframes, and the Otsu with a teardrop canopy and cut down fuselage identical to the Ki-61-II Kai. To improve the high-altitude performance of the Ki-100 work had begun on a more potent version fitted with an Ha-112-II Ru engine that incorporated an Ru-102-II turbo-supercharger and water-methanol injection. The Japanese struggle to perfect a reliable turbo-supercharger for fighter use centred mainly on problems with the manufacture of a suitable steel or substitute alloy for the exhaust gas turbines.

As designed, the Ki-100-II would have been the lightest turbo-supercharged fighter of World War 2. The first of three prototypes built for testing made its maiden flight in May 1945, and the fighter's ability to attain its optimum speed at an altitude of just over 26,000 ft was an improvement on the standard Ki-100. Even so, turbo-supercharger issues delayed production and the war ended before Ki-100-IIs could reach the frontline.

APPENDIX II

LEADING Ki-61 AND Ki-100 ACES*

Rank	Name	Unit	Victories
Capt	Shogo Takeuchi	68th Sentai	46 (including damaged and probables)
1Lt	Mitsuyoshi Tarui	68th Sentai	38
1Lt	Shogo Saito	78th Sentai	26+**
Sgt	Susumu Kajinami	68th Sentai	24 (including 16 probables)
WO	Tokuyasu Ishizuka	78th Sentai	23
Capt	Saburo Togo	6th Rensei Hikotai	22
WO	Kazuo Shimizu	59th Sentai	18
1Lt	Keiji Takamiya	78th Sentai	17
Sgt Maj	Tomio Hirohata	59th Sentai	14
Capt	Nagao Shirai	244th Sentai	13 (11 B-29s)
Capt	Totaro Ito	5th Sentai	13+ (9+ B-29s)
WO	Takashi Noguchi	68th Sentai	12 (14 claimed)
Maj	Yohei Hinoki	Akeno/111th Sentai	12 (1 B-29)
Capt	Junichi Ogata	56th Sentai	12 (4 B-29s)
Capt	Chuichi Ichikawa	78th/244th Sentais	10 (9 B-29s)
MSgt	Jiro Asano	244th Sentai	10
1Lt	Hiroshi Sekiguchi	68th Sentai	7
1Lt	Mitsusada Asai	78th Sentai	7
Capt	Fumisuke Shono	244th Sentai	6
WO	Tadao Sumi	56th Sentai	6 (5 B-29s)
Maj	Teruhiko Kobayashi	244th Sentai	5 (3 B-29s)***
Sgt	Matsumi Nakano	244th Sentai	5 (3 B-29s)
2Lt	Kesashige Ogata	55th Sentai	5
1Lt	Naoyuki Ogata	59th Sentai	5 (3 B-29s)
1Lt	Takashi Tomishima	78th Sentai	4+
Capt	Haruo Kawamura	18th Sentai	4 B-29s (+5 damaged)
Capt	Mitsuo Oyake	18th Sentai	4 B-29s
1Lt	Minoru Shirota	55th Sentai	4 B-29s
2Lt	Takeo Adachi	55th Sentai	4 B-29s
2Lt	Katsumi Hattori	244th Sentai	4 B-29s

* Includes aces who made claims flying other types but completed their careers flying the Ki-61 and/or Ki-100
** One confirmed B-24 flying the Hien
*** Some sources include damaged claims for a total of 12, with 10 B-29s

Ki-61-I Ko

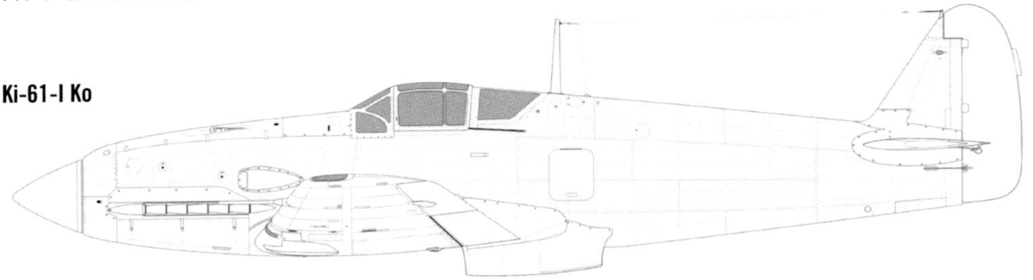

Ki-61-I Otsu

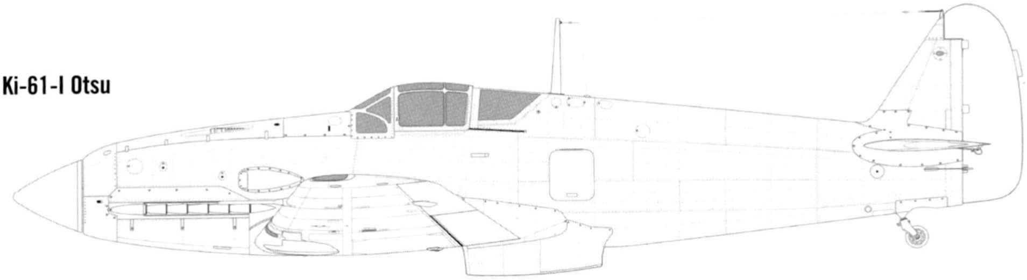

Ki-61-I Hei

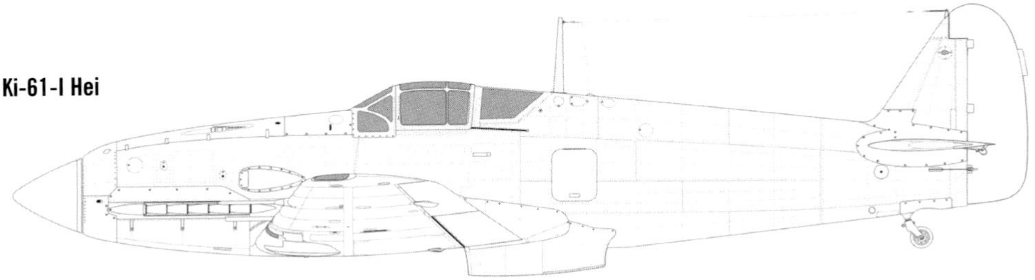

Ki-61-I Tei

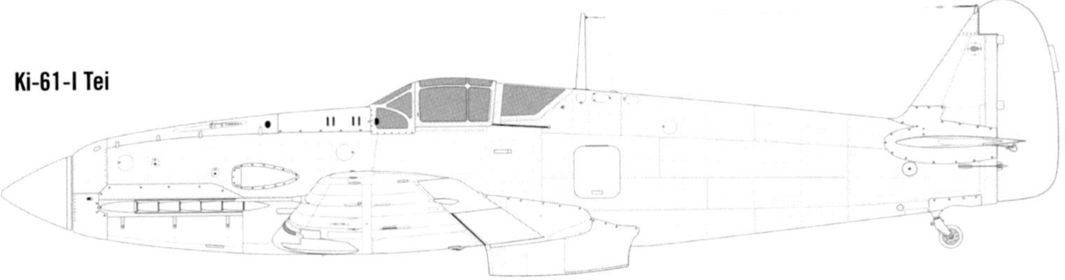

Ki-100-I Ko

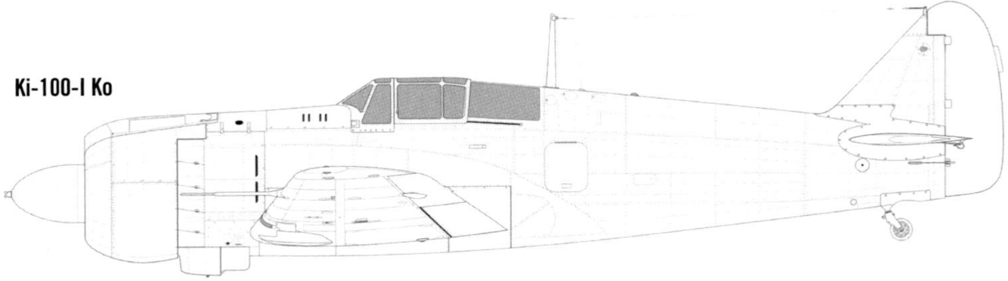

Ki-100-I Otsu

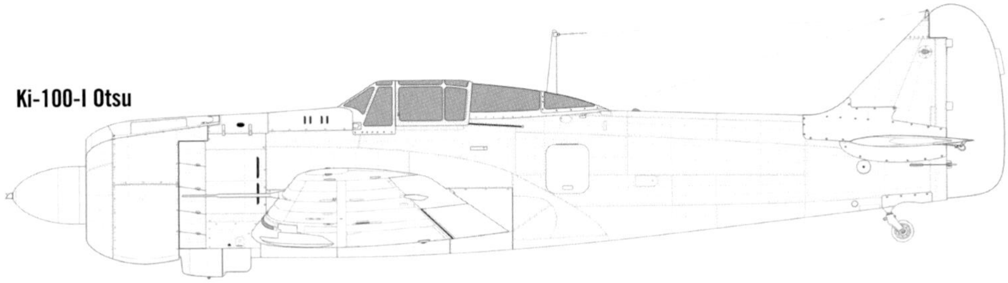

All line drawings are to 1/72nd scale

COLOUR PLATES

1

Ki-61 second prototype serial number 6102 flown by Maj Yoshitsugu Aramaki, Mito, Japan, April 1942

Maj Aramaki flew this aircraft in an abortive attempt to intercept B-25 bombers during the Doolittle Raid on Tokyo. He was instrumental in testing the Ki-61 at the Army Air Test Centre at Fussa, and later commanded the 17th Sentai in the Philippines. In contrast to production aircraft, which had dark brown painted propellers and spinners, only the rear face of each blade was painted dark brown on this aircraft. Note the additional windows in front of the windscreen. The anti-glare panel is koku ran shoku (black indigo), which is a blueish black. The fabric control surfaces, rudder, elevators and ailerons on production aircraft were usually finished in either aluminium or greenish grey dope.

2

Ki-61-I Ko serial number 388 of Sgt Susumu Kajinami, 2nd Chutai, 68th Sentai, Kagimigahara, Japan, September 1943

Sgt Kajinami was allocated this Hien in July 1943 and he flew it to New Guinea from Japan. Before departure the fighter was camouflaged with a dark green 'snake weave' (there was no standard pattern), and it had a white band – the war front sign senchi hiyoshiki – or so-called combat stripe painted around the rear fuselage. On arrival in New Guinea this aircraft was assigned to another pilot. Sgt Kajinami claimed eight victories and 16 damaged during the New Guinea campaign.

3

Ki-61-I Ko serial number 263 of Capt Shogo Takeuchi, 2nd Chutai leader, 68th Sentai, Cape Gloucester, New Britain, September 1943

This Hien, captured almost intact at Tuluvu airstrip in December 1943, has been attributed to both Takeuchi and Mitsuyoshi Tarui. Often depicted with a neat red border to the white fuselage band, the latter had in fact been painted over a dark band. This had perhaps been applied when the aircraft changed hands, with the dark paint still showing at the edges. The detachment at Cape Gloucester was from the 2nd Chutai, and as leader, Takeuchi's command band should have been red. A 'Tony' from this detachment photographed at Vunakanau, on Rabaul, on 12 October 1943 also appears to have a white fuselage band. The red colour shown in the profile is speculative. The aircraft had a single 'eagle' victory marking beneath the cockpit, whereas some sources assert that Takeuchi's Hien was adorned with 58 eagle wing victory markings.

4

Ki-61-I Ko '56' of Sgt Iwao Tabata, 3rd Chutai, 68th Sentai, Wewak, New Guinea, Late 1943

Sgt Tabata flew as the second 'rotte' (pair) leader in 3rd Chutai leader Lt Akenori Motoyama's Shotai. He was shot down near Wewak on 22 December 1943 but survived the experience following a four-day trek through the jungle. Tabata later flew as an instructor with the 39th Kyoiku Hikotai in the air defence of Japan, flying the open cockpit Ki-79 trainer in combat and later the Hien. He shared two fighter kills and two damaged B-29s with his regular wingman Sgt Shoichi Kaiho (see Profile 33). Tabata'a 68th Sentai Hien is reproduced here from a description he gave in an interview in 1969.

5

Ki-61-I Ko '15' of the 1st Chutai, 68th Sentai, Dagua, New Guinea, February 1944

The simple diagonal 'spear head' marking on the tail fin and rudder of this Hien, which appears to be in white, has been attributed as a later 68th Sentai insignia, perhaps introduced to simplify painting. Seen applied to aircraft before the two Hien units were amalgamated in March 1944, it was unlikely to represent a new combined marking. Some 68th Sentai aircraft displayed a two-digit number at the top of the rudder, as here. The spinner on this aircraft was white, with the exception of the back plate, and the diagonal white fuselage band indicates either a Chutai or, more probably, a Shotai leader. At this time the 1st Chutai leader was Capt Toshio Takenawa.

6

Ki-61-I Ko 'Ki' '19' of the 78th Sentai, Boram, New Guinea, October 1943

This Hien was photographed on the ground at Boram during an aerial attack by Allied bombers. The bands on the fin and tailplanes have been attributed as the markings used by the 78th Sentai in New Guinea, and they appear to be white in this case. The tip of the spinner also appears to be white. The rudder displays the Katakana character 'Ki' and '19' is painted on the wheel cover – probably the last two digits of the aircraft's serial number, which would make it a Ko manufactured in March, June or August 1943.

7

Ki-61-I of the 78th Sentai, Dagua, New Guinea, February 1944

Individual markings cannot be attributed to the notable pilots of the 78th Sentai, while the distinctive markings of the unit remain enigmatic. There is a general pattern of single bands of colour on the tail fin and tailplanes, observed in red, yellow and white, as well as blue, sometimes combined with one or more stripes on the rudder that perhaps represent the Shotai. Aircraft spinners or spinner tips appear to be painted in Chutai colours.

8

Ki-61-I unit unknown, Dagua, New Guinea, February 1944

This unusual Hien with a tail marking not typical of either the 68th or 78th Sentais was photographed at Dagua during a raid on 3 February 1944. The painted rudder tip was perhaps a form of command marking. There was possibly the Kana character 'Ne' painted on the rudder, but it is not entirely legible. The colour of the tail marking and spinner are presumed to be white, but might have been yellow. Both Sentais are reported to have used the usual Chutai colour sequence of white, red and yellow for the 1st, 2nd and 3rd Chutais, with blue as the Sentai Hombu colour. However, an early reference gives the 78th sequence as non-standard red, yellow and green (or blue).

9

Ki-61-I Otsu 'Wa' of the 78th Sentai, Wasile, Halmaheras, early 1944

Some aircraft from both Sentais had single Katakana characters painted on the rudder with or without other markings and sometimes within a circular border. Whilst those might be abbreviated names of pilots assigned to the aircraft, they could also be markings applied for ferrying purposes. This aircraft is one of a batch of reinforcement Hiens ferried to Wasile shortly before the campaign ended, and it has the character 'Wa' on the rudder but no other distinguishing markings. The constant attrition of aircraft and flow of replacements made it unlikely that any coherent system of marking could be maintained, and the probability is that the majority of recorded markings represent the vestiges of previously more ordered systems and/or ad hoc tactical markings applied to serve immediate needs.

10
Ki-61-I Tei of Capt Takefumi Yano, 55th Sentai, Komaki, Japan, summer 1944

Capt Yano was the 1st Chutai leader and acting CO of the unit in the Philippines after Maj Shigeo Iwahashi was killed there in November 1944. He too did not return to Japan, being killed in action in January 1945. His Hien is painted in the solid late-war scheme of olive brown with unpainted undersurfaces and a cobalt blue command band. The unit had not yet adopted an insignia, and the Kanji symbol on the fin is 'Ya' for his name – it also meant 'arrow'.

11
Ki-61-I Otsu of 1Lt Takumi Fukui, 2nd Chutai, 50th Sentai, Heho, Burma, March 1944

The 50th Sentai briefly evaluated the Hien in Burma during March and April 1944, with 1Lt Fukui (the acting 2nd Chutai leader) collecting the first example from Singapore. This Hien, named 'Masa' (Prosperous), was destroyed on the ground at Aungban on 4 April 1944. Although a second Ki-61 was received and selected groundcrew were given training on the type, the 'Tony' was considered unsuitable for operations from the rough and ready airfields of Burma. The 50th Sentai re-equipped with the more rugged Ki-84 Hayate instead.

12
Ki-61-I of WO Takeo Tagata, Rensei Boukutai No 1, 8th Rensei Hikotai, Heito, Taiwan, October 1944

The appearance of this Hien in an ad hoc air defence unit is speculative, based on a painting and the insignia of the parent unit. Tagata and his wingman fought an epic battle with US Navy Hellcats on 12 October 1944, the former claiming to have destroyed or damaged 11 before having to force land his badly shot up and burning Hien. Tagata's claims are not borne out by US Navy records, however, although the naval aviators involved acknowledged an engagement with highly skilled IJAAF pilots that resulted in the loss of four Hellcats.

13
Ki-61-I Tei of 2Lt Takeo Adachi, 55th Sentai, Komaki, Japan, December 1944

Adachi flew this unpainted Hien as part of the 55th Sentai's base detachment of nine pilots who remained in Japan as a training cadre and participated in air defence duties. It had been adorned with four claims for B-29s by the time Adachi was killed in action on 19 January 1945. The presentation of the tail marking is speculative as it is not in view in the only known photograph of the aircraft.

14
Ki-61-I Tei '24' of Capt Teruhiko Kobayashi, 244th Sentai Hombu, Hamamatsu, Japan, December 1944

Hien serial number 4424 (manufactured in July 1944) was flown by Kobayashi with various marking changes, and it is depicted here as flown by the ace during the period from December 1944 to January 1945. Victory markings for one B-29 destroyed (solid planform) and three damaged (silhouettes) are displayed beneath the cockpit. It was delivered in natural metal finish and camouflaged with dense but crudely daubed blotches of dark green. The wing armament was removed in order to improve the fighter's high-altitude performance.

15
Ki-61-I Hei '295' of Capt Teruhiko Kobayashi, 244th Sentai Hombu, Chofu, Japan, January 1945

Kobayashi inherited Hien serial number 3295 from the 1st Chutai leader, Capt Toyohisa Komatsu, and had the tail painted and the broad white stripe added for recognition. The fuselage Hinomaru is shown here correctly with a white border for the first time. The fighter was manufactured in April 1944 before the introduction of factory painting, being camouflaged in the field with dark green mottle over natural metal. It is believed Kobayashi flew '295' on 27 January 1945 when it was destroyed ramming or colliding with a B-29, as his regular '24' was out of service for maintenance. Note the venturi below the windscreen, reportedly for a new type of gyro gunsight, although photographs appear to show the fighter fitted with a standard Type 100 gunsight.

16
Ki-61-I Tei '24' of Capt Teruhiko Kobayashi, 244th Sentai Hombu, Chofu, Japan, February 1945

This is serial number 4424 as photographed in February 1945 with the crude camouflage removed and the fuselage stripe re-painted blue. Some modern depictions show the command stripe and rear fuselage band as red. However, after examination of original photographs and careful consideration of the evidence for red, we have decided to revert to blue in accordance with earlier references. Blue was also the recognised Sentai Hombu and command colour distinction in the IJAAF. The radio antenna mast and cockpit head armour have by now been removed from the aircraft, and the wings remain devoid of weaponry. The fighter's kill markings include a fifth B-29 and Kobayashi's ramming victory from 27 January 1945.

17
Ki-61-I Tei '24' of Capt Teruhiko Kobayashi, 244th Sentai Hombu, Chofu, Japan, March 1945

Serial number 4424 is depicted here as it was flown by Kobayashi on Shimbu-tai escort missions during March 1945. The Hien had by then been re-camouflaged with dark green mottle, and the white Kanji characters 'hitsu sho' (sure to prevail) were painted on the rudder and the front of the underwing drop tanks, not seen here. The wing leading edge identification friend or foe strips have been depicted in the past in red, and whilst they appear dark in one photograph, another shot taken on the same day suggests they were the usual yellow. Wing armament appears to have been refitted. When Kobayashi began flying the Ki-100, this aircraft was presented to the leader of the 159th Shimbu-tai, 2Lt Shunzo Takashima, who had been his student at Akeno – the 159th was formed from within the 244th on 26 April. On 6 June Takashima departed Chiran in this famous Hien on a one-way flight, for it was never seen again.

18
Ki-61-I Tei '62' of Capt Teruhiko Kobayashi, 244th Sentai Hombu, Chofu, Japan, April 1945

This olive brown painted Hien (serial number 5262) was flown by 2Lt Yujiro Itakura whilst escorting the 19th Shimbu-tai on 19 March 1945. It was re-painted in preparation for assignment to Kobayashi as a reserve aircraft after he was wounded on 12 April 1945. When he returned to duty, Kobayashi began flying the Ki-100, so it is unlikely that this aircraft was ever flown by him in combat. Serial number 5262 was manufactured in November 1944 after the introduction of factory painting.

19
Ki-61-I Tei '87', 244th Sentai, Akeno, Japan, April 1945
This mystery aircraft is reported to have been the last Hien flown by Kobayashi, and it was photographed by Mamoru Tatsuda of the 111th Sentai at Akeno in April 1945. However, although it appears to display Kobayashi's victory tally (with apparent errors in the order), the date and identity of the pilot are disputed. The dark stripe visible in Tatsuda's photograph has been variously depicted as blue, red or over-painted, and the tail is not visible. The white stripe on the antenna mast was usually the mark of a fledgling pilot in the 244th, which only adds to the mystery.

20
Ki-61-I Otsu '33' of Cpl Matsumi Nakano, 244th Sentai Shinten Seikutai, Chofu, Japan, December 1944
Cpl Nakano of the 244th's Shinten Seikutai air-to-air ramming flight intercepted a box-formation of 12 B-29s in this unarmed Hien on 3 December 1944. After two failures in approach, he made a third dive on a B-29 in the centre of the box but missed it, ending up beneath the bomber. After a few seconds of level flight he zoomed up at full throttle and tore into one of the tailplanes with his propeller. At first the B-29 climbed, with the Hien still caught in the tailplane, but then it began to fall and the Hien was freed to belly-land safely. The damaged Ki-61 was displayed outside Tokyo's Matsuya Department Store over Christmas, together with a full scale mock-up of a B-29 and parts recovered from a crashed example. On 27 January 1945 Nakano, now promoted to sergeant, was flying with Sgt Masao Itagaki, who had also survived two ramming attacks, when they intercepted a formation of ten B-29s. Nakano dived, missed the B-29, zoomed up and tore off its tail, before again performing a successful belly landing.

21
Ki-61-I Ko '16' of Sgt Matsumi Nakano, 244th Sentai Shinten Seikutai, Chofu, Japan, February 1945
This unarmed Hien, painted dark green and variously reported to be a Ko or Otsu, was adorned with Nakano's three B-29 claims, two by ramming. Sgts Nakano and Itagaki served in the Shinten Seikutai until it was disbanded on 10 March 1945, each man surviving two successful B-29 ramming attacks to the adulation of other members of the unit. The Katakana character on the rudder is 'Na' for Nakano. Itagaki's Hien '14', otherwise identical, displayed the character 'I' (Yi) and had a white rear fuselage band.

22
Ki-61-I Hei '15' of Cpl Seichi Suzuki, Mikazuki-tai, 244th Sentai, Hamamatsu, Japan, January 1945
The 20-year-old Suzuki's Mauser-armed Hien displayed elaborate kill markings for his B-29 claims – a shared claim with Capt Shirai on 22 December 1944, two shared claims on 3 January 1945, a single-handed claim on 9 January, a damaged on 14 January and two shared damaged on 27 January. Suzuki then flew with the Sentai Hombu until he was killed in combat with US Navy Task Force 58 carrier fighters during his fifth sortie of the day on 16 February 1945.

23
Ki-61-I Otsu '16' of Capt Fumisuke Shono, Soyokaze-tai Leader, 244th Sentai, Hamamatsu, January 1945
This Hien with three victory symbols is less well known than Capt Shono's '88' with its fuselage lightning bolt. Although the wing armament is typical of a Ki-61-I Otsu, this aircraft appears to reveal the serial number 316 on a wing root stencil in one of several good photographs that survive on it, suggesting that the fighter may have originally been a Ki-61-I Ko. Capt Shono was the leader of the Soyokaze-tai, and he ended the war with six victory claims to his name, including two P-51s shot down whilst flying a Ki-100 during his final sortie on 16 July 1945.

24
Ki-61-I '57' of 2Lt Shoichi Takayama, 5th Shinten Seikutai, 244th Sentai, Chofu, Japan, January 1945
The 21-year-old 2Lt Shoichi Takayama was put in charge of the Shinten Seikutai in December 1944 when its former leader 1Lt Touru Shinomiya took command of the 19th Shimbu-tai. He survived ramming a B-29 on 9 January 1945, for which he was awarded an Army Command commendation and the Bukosho, but was killed when he hit a second bomber on 27 January. For that attack Takayama was awarded an individual citation and posthumously promoted to captain. Although the aircraft in the profile has been attributed to Takayama by at least two sources this cannot be definitely confirmed. Indeed, the character 'Ta' on the tail might also refer to Lt Mitsuyuki Tange, another Shinten Seikutai pilot who was killed ramming a B-29 on 9 January 1945.

25
Ki-61-I Hei of 1Lt Mitsuo Oyake, 18th Sentai (6th Shinten Seikutai), Kashiwa, Japan, January 1945
This profile of Oyake's Hei is based on a partial photograph that clearly shows the style of victory marking, together with a description of how the tail was painted all red in similar fashion to other 10th Air Division Shinten Seikutai flights, with the 'darts' of the 18th's unit emblem in white. Although Oyake had proposed the formation of an air-to-air ramming unit in the 18th, and made a successful ramming attack himself on 7 April 1945, thereby claiming his fourth B-29, it is not known if he was flying this armed Hei adorned with his three previous B-29 claims when he took his tally to four.

26
Ki-61-I Tei '50' of 2nd Chutai, 55th Sentai, Sano, Japan, August 1945
This anonymous late production Tei, photographed in a line-up of the 55th Sentai's 20 remaining Hiens at Sano at war's end, reveals previous ownership by the 59th Sentai. The 59th had converted to the Ki-100 in May, relinquishing most of its remaining Hiens to other units. After disastrous experiences in the Philippines and at Okinawa that resulted in the loss of two commanding officers and three Hikotai/Chutai leaders, as well as most of its pilots, the 55th Sentai changed its tail insignia from the earlier form shown in Profile 13 to that shown here. The only known five-victory ace of the unit was 2Lt Kesashige Ogata, who claimed five P-38s. The 55th ended the war under the direct command of the 11th Air Division as part of the permanently stationed air defence forces in the Central Sector of Japan, the Sentai being one of only two remaining Hien units of any strength.

27
Ki-61-1 Hei serial number 3294 of the 56th Sentai, Itami, Japan, December 1944
Some sources assert that because it was organised on a Hikotai basis with a single Hikotai leader, the 56th Sentai insignia was not distinguished by Chutai colours but was always painted red on natural metal aircraft and white on camouflaged aircraft, although it is also sometimes shown as yellow on the latter. Each aircraft also displayed the last three digits of its serial number on the lower rudder. The distinguishing markings, if any, and aircraft numbers of the 56th's two aces, Capt Junichi Ogata and WO Tadao Sumi, are unknown.

28
Ki-61-1 Tei '751' of Maj Yaruyoshi Furukawa, 56th Sentai, Itami, Japan, December 1944
The white Homeland Defence 'bandages' on the fuselage of Maj Furukawa's factory-painted Hien (manufactured in August 1944) were unique, and were said to distinguish him as the Sentai commander. Two authoritative sources record the spinner of the factory-painted Tei as being in the same olive brown camouflage as the airframe, although it is usually depicted in the earlier dark brown.

29
Ki-100 Otsu of Capt Teruhiko Kobayashi, 244th Sentai Hombu, Chiran, Japan, May 1945
The only known photograph of Kobayashi's Ki-100, taken on 17 May 1945, does not show the tail unit, but it appears unlikely that it was painted red. The fuselage band has usually been depicted as yellow, but it was more likely cobalt blue – the recognised command colour – as shown here, conforming to previous unit practice. This aircraft had a short life, being written off in a taxiing accident just after arriving at Chiran from Miyakonojo.

30
Ki-100 Otsu of Maj Yohei Hinoki, 2nd Daitai, Akeno Kyodo Hikoshidan and 111th Sentai, Akeno, Japan, July 1945
This profile is recreated from a coloured drawing annotated by Maj Hinoki himself. The uppersurface of the wings had diagonal cobalt blue bands outlined in white to commemorate Hinoki's former commander in the 64th Sentai, Maj Tateo Kato. The aircraft number is speculative, as although Hinoki recalled that a two-digit number was painted on the lower rudder and wheel covers, he could not remember what it was. The tail tip is the marking of the 111th Sentai, and it might not have been worn when the Ki-100 was being flown as part of the Kyodo Hikoshidan. It was supposed to be in the Chutai colour, and as Maj Hinoki commanded the 2nd Daitai (4th and 5th Chutai) it seems unlikely that it was white (for the 1st Chutai) as is usually shown.

31
Ki-100 Ko of Maj Toyoki Eto, 1st Daitai, Akeno Kyodo Hikoshidan and 111th Sentai, Akeno, Japan, July 1945
Maj Eto commanded the 1st Daitai of the 111th Sentai (1st, 2nd and 3rd Chutais), and this profile is based on a photograph of an aircraft attributed to him. The three bands to the rear of the Hinomaru are usually depicted in white, but they might have been yellow. The colour of this aircraft is sometimes depicted as black, and referred to as 'charcoal', but the Japanese term describing the colour – kuro kasshoku – means 'blackish brown', and probably refers to a particularly dark olive drab found on some batches of Ki-100 Ko. This was a colour close to RAL 6014 Gelbolive (Yellow olive).

32
Ki-100 Otsu of 1Lt Mamoru Tatsuda, Akeno Kyodo Hikoshidan and 111th Sentai, Akeno, Japan, July 1945
Another colourful Goshikisen from Akeno's 'kettle of hawks', this machine was flown by 1Lt Mamoru Tatsuda. By the end of the war the 111th Sentai had 90 Ki-100s on strength, although the number of skilled and experienced pilots available to fly them was considerably less than that. The elaborate markings system of coloured bands and tail flashes found on the Ki-100s at Akeno has never been deciphered.

33
Ki-100 Otsu of Capt Totaro Ito, 3rd Chutai, 5th Sentai, Kiyosi, Japan, summer 1945
According to Capt Saito, the 5th Sentai received a batch of Ki-100s that were painted 'dark green', whereas the Ki-100s issued to the 18th Sentai were painted 'ohryuku nana go shoku' (yellow green No 7 colour) – the late-war olive drab colour. Capt Ito accumulated his score of 13+ victories (including at least nine B-29s) flying the Ki-45, Ki-61 (reportedly) and Ki-100. He was awarded the Bukosho for his successes. Ito had the Kanji characters for 'Nine Headed Dragon' painted on the rudder of all of his aircraft, possibly in memory of a temple near his birthplace in Fukui Prefecture. The 5th Sentai's tail insignia was not distinguished by Chutai, but the spinner tip was painted in the Chutai colour – in this case red for the 3rd Chutai.

34
Ki-61-I Otsu '22' of Sgt Shuichi Kaiho, 39th Rensei Hikotai, Yokoshiba, Japan, July 1945
The Hien of 20-year-old Sgt Kaiho had the cowling guns removed, but the troughs were not faired over. It also had cartridge collection blisters under the wings. The red tail symbol was not outlined in white, as is often depicted, but the 'border' was the natural metal finish of the aircraft. The solid-painted Hien '21' of Kaiho's 'rotte' leader, Sgt Iwao Tabata, which bore identical victory markings, is better known. Their accumulated victories were painted on both aircraft.

35
Ki-100 Ko serial number 16153 of the 3rd Chutai, 59th Sentai, Ashiya, Japan, October 1945
This profile is based on a photograph taken at Ashiya after the war. Probably because of the P-51 kill marking, serial number 16153 has been identified as the aircraft of the 3rd Chutai leader, and Bukosho winner, 1Lt Naoyuki Ogata, who claimed five victories (including three B-29s). Close examination of original prints reveals that the distinctive 59th Sentai span-wise Chutai colour tailplane bands between the stabiliser and elevator *were* painted on the Ki-100.

36
Ki-100 Ko of Capt Haruo Kawamura, 3rd Chutai Leader, 18th Sentai, Matsudo, Japan, August 1945
Capt Kawamura either collided with or rammed a B-29 in this aircraft on the night of 1 August 1945 after twice attacking it with gunfire. He was able to parachute to safety and survived the encounter. The bomber was his fourth B-29 destroyed, with claims for a further five damaged.

BIBLIOGRAPHY

Ferguson, S W and Pascalis, William K, *Protect & Avenge (49th FG in World War 2)*, Schiffer, 1996

Goodwin, Mike, *Japanese Aero-Engines 1930-1945*, JASIG, 2002

Hata, Ikuhiko, Izawa, Yasuho and Shores, Christopher, *Japanese Army Air Force Fighter Units and their Aces 1931-1945*, Grub Street, 2002

Hickey, Lawrence J, *Warpath across the Pacific*, International Research and Publishing Corporation, 1984

Janowicz, Krzysztof, *68 Sentai*, Kagero, 2003

Japan Defence Agency, *Army Air Operations in Southeast Asia*, Asagumo Shimbunsha, 1970

Kanzaki, Col Kiyoshi and others, *Homeland Air Defence Operations Record, HQ USAFFE and 8th Army*, Tokyo, 1958

Lambert, John W, *The Pineapple Air Force*, Phalanx, 1990

Mann, Robert A, *The B-29 Superfortress*, McFarland, 1997

Matsumae, Col, *4th Air Army Operations 1944-1945*, 1st Demobilisation Bureau, 1946

McAulay, Lex, *MacArthur's Eagles*, Naval Institute Press, 2005

Military Analysis Division, *Japanese Air Weapons and Tactics*, USSBS, 1947

Mizumachi, Lt Col and Takayama, Maj, *Air Operation Record of Iwo Island and the Southwestern Islands from Japan Proper (The 6th Army Air Force)*, 1st Demobilisation Bureau, 1946

Morse, Cdr J H, *Kawasaki Engine Design and Development*, ATIG, FEAF, 1945

Nohara, Shigeru, *Kawasaki Ki-61 Hien*, Model Art, 2006

Nomaka, Col, *Southeast Area Air Operations Record, July 1942-June 1944*, 1st Demobilisation Bureau, 1946

Pennings, Marco and Oedenrode, Sint, *Lahirnya Angkatan Udara Republik Indonesia*, self-published 2006

Picarella, Giuseppe, *Kawasaki Ki-100 Goshiki-Sentouki*, Dainippon Kaiga, 2009

Rielly, Robin L, *Kamikaze Attacks of World War II*, McFarland, 2010

Rudge, Chris, *Air-To-Air (The story behind the air-to-air combat claims of the RNZAF)*, self-published, 2003

Sakaida, Henry, *Pacific Air Combat World War 2*, Phalanx, 1993

Sakaida, Henry, *Osprey Aircraft of the Aces 13 – Japanese Army Air Force Aces 1937-45*, Osprey 1997

Sakurai, Takashi, *Hien*, Dainippon Kaiga, 2004

Sato, Lt Col Katsuo, *Air Operations Record against Soviet Russia, HQ Army Forces Far East*, 1952

Shiba, Maj Takira and others, *Air Defence of the Homeland, Japanese Monograph No 23, HQ USAFFE and 8th Army*, Tokyo, 1956

Stanaway, John, *Cobra in the Clouds, Historical Aviation Album*, 1982

Stanaway, John, *Kearby's Thunderbolts (348th FG in World War 2)*, Phalanx, 1992

Stanaway, John, Possum, *Clover & Hades (475th FG in World War 2)*, Schiffer, 1993

Stanaway, John and Hickey, Lawrence J, *Attack & Conquer (8th FG in World War 2)*, Schiffer, 1995

Tanaka, Koji, *Record of Southeast Pacific Operations Part 4 Air Force Operations*, ATIS, 1946

Takaki, Koji and Sakaida, Henry, *Osprey Aviation Elite Units 5 – B-29 Hunters of the JAAF*, Osprey, 2001

Watanabe, Yohji, *Pictorial History of Air War Over Japan - JAAF*, Hara Shobo, 1980

Watanabe, Yohji, *Army Fighter Ki-61*, Hara Shobo, 1983

Werrell, Kenneth P, *Blankets of Fire – US Bombers over Japan during World War II*, Smithsonian Institution, 1996

INDEX

locators in **bold** refer to illustrations, captions
and plates.